# THE REBEL GIRLS HANDBOOK

PACKED WITH FACTS AND ACTIVITIES ABOUT 300+ EXTRAORDINARY WOMEN

Good Night Stories for Rebel Girls and Rebel Girls are registered trademarks.

Good Night Stories for Rebel Girls and all other Rebel Girls titles are available for bulk purchase for sale promotions, premiums, fundraising, and educational needs. For details, write to sales@rebelgirls.com.

www.rebelgirls.com

Art director: Giulia Flamini

Design: Georgena Senor, Kristen Brittain, Nicky Collings

Contributors: Gina Grandi, Grace Srinivasiah, Jess Harriton, Joe Rhatigan, Maithy Vu, Sarah Parvis, Sofía Aguilar, Sydnee Monday

Special thanks: Marina Asenjo

Library of Congress Control Number: 2022938035

Rebel Girls, Inc.
421 Elm Ave.
Larkspur, CA 94939

Printed in Dubai
First Edition: May 2022
10 9 8 7 6 5 4 3 2 1
ISBN: 978-1-953424-30-3

# CONTENTS

# INTRODUCTION

Rebel Girls are bold and daring.

Rebel Girls are kind and compassionate.

Rebel Girls are clever and curious and adventurous and ambitious and determined.

They sing, dance, and soar through the skies. They invent, innovate, and fight for justice.

Throughout this book, you will meet girls and women from all over the world and throughout history.

You will read about their lives, their accomplishments, their quirky habits, and even their pets. And you'll uncover some of their superpowers—the traits and talents that help them be resilient and make their mark on the world. As you flip through these pages, think about what you do well, what makes your heart sing, and how you can support the Rebel Girls in your life.

Earth needs more Rebels.
Welcome to the team!

# BE ON THE LOOKOUT FOR CODES LIKE THIS!

When you find them, scan them with your phone and you'll be transported to the Rebel Girls app, where you can hear stories about the incredible women in the Rebel Girls universe.

# HOW TO USE THIS BOOK

Flip through the first section of the book to see where many Rebel Girls come from. Some pages show entire continents.

Other pages shine a spotlight on a particular country.

Another chapter shows a timeline of Rebel Girls, from thousands of years ago to just the other day. See how the actions of Rebel Women fit together with some of the other major events on Earth, like the building of the Great Pyramids or the invention of the World Wide Web.

Most of the pages in this book highlight specific Rebel Girls, calling out where they are from, when they lived, and what makes them memorable.

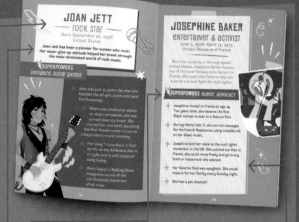

- At the top of each page, you will find the Rebel Girl's name, a description of her job or what she does best, her birth and death dates, and the country or countries where she was born and/or did her inspiring work.

- Here's a short description of why this woman has landed in the Rebel Girls Hall of Fame.

- Rebels are a multitalented bunch (just like you!), and we've called out some of the traits and talents that help them dream big and crush their goals.

- Learn more about each Rebel!

- Whenever you see the words YOUR TURN!, you'll know there is a fun activity for you to try out.

- Some pages show pictures of the Rebel Girl. Does she look like you thought she would?

# REBEL GIRLS AROUND THE WORLD

Rebel Girls are everywhere!
Explore these maps to discover incredible
innovators, leaders, creators, and
champions from all over the world.

# NORTH AMERICA

North America extends from the snowy island of Greenland all the way to sunny Panama. In all 23 countries that make up this continent, women have accomplished many remarkable things. In the late 1800s, Matilde Montoya became the first female doctor in Mexico. Later, in Cuba, Alicia Alonso fulfilled her dream of becoming a ballet dancer even when an eye condition made her partially blind. And in the United States, Simone Biles earned the title of most decorated gymnast in the world for her gravity-defying flips and flawless balance beam routines.

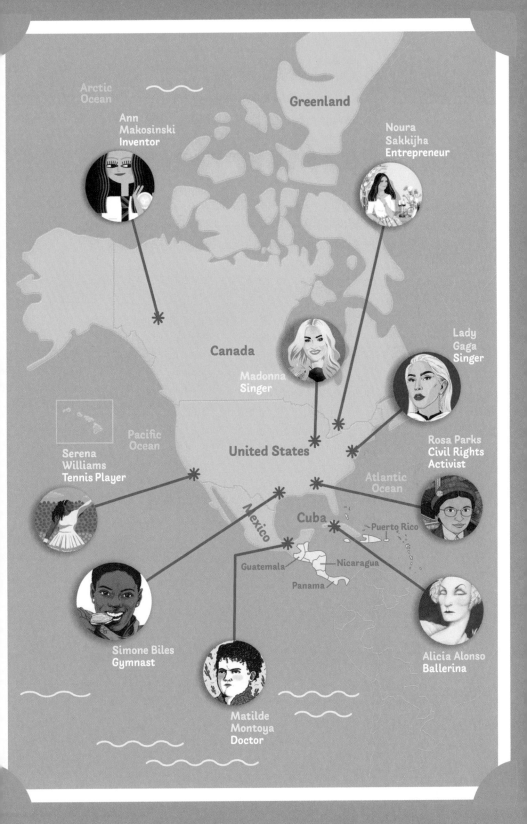

Arctic Ocean

Greenland

Ann Makosinski
Inventor

Noura Sakkijha
Entrepreneur

Lady Gaga
Singer

Canada

Madonna
Singer

Pacific Ocean

Serena Williams
Tennis Player

United States

Rosa Parks
Civil Rights Activist

Atlantic Ocean

Mexico

Cuba

Puerto Rico

Guatemala

Nicaragua

Panama

Simone Biles
Gymnast

Matilde Montoya
Doctor

Alicia Alonso
Ballerina

# CANADA

Canada's vast lands include dense forests, snowy Arctic regions, and deep blue lakes and rivers. It spans six time zones! Amazing women have come from all over the country.

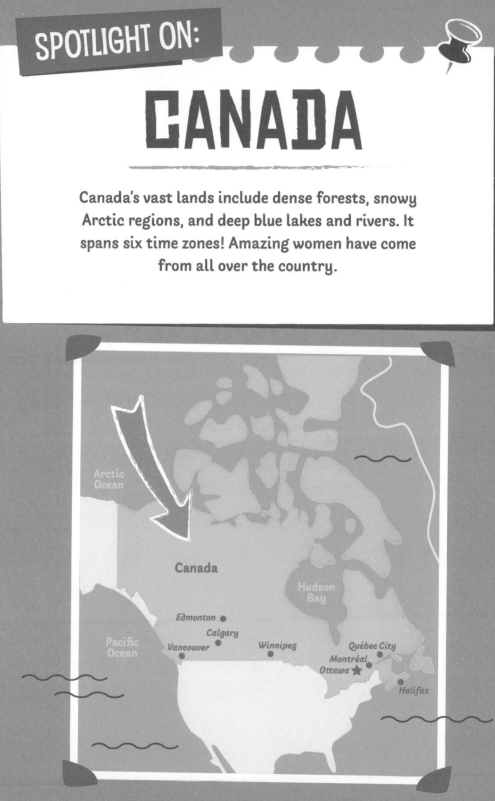

Arctic Ocean

Canada

Hudson Bay

Pacific Ocean

Edmonton
Calgary
Vancouver
Winnipeg
Québec City
Montréal
Ottawa ★
Halifax

## BRIGETTE LACQUETTE

Hockey player Brigette Lacquette grew up in a small Indigenous community near one of Canada's enormous lakes, Lake Winnipeg.

## MARGARET ATWOOD

Deep in the woods of Ottawa, author Margaret Atwood spent her childhood making up fantastical stories. Even then, she was on her way to her future career as a best-selling novelist.

## VIOLA DESMOND

In the seaside city of Halifax, Viola Desmond realized there were no hair salons just for Black women. So she started her own. Later, she stood up for herself by refusing to give up her seat in a movie theater that discriminated against Black people.

# SPOTLIGHT ON:

# MEXICO

Mexico is a country of contrasting landscapes. Mountains roll through the central region, lush rain forests sprawl in the south, and dry deserts stretch toward California in the north. Many talented women have contributed to the vibrant culture of Mexico.

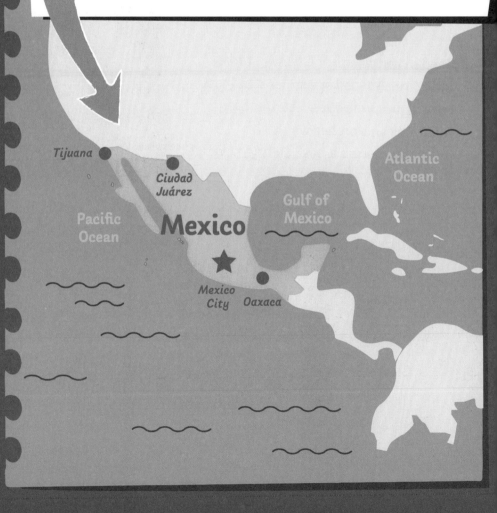

Tijuana

Ciudad Juárez

Atlantic Ocean

Gulf of Mexico

Pacific Ocean

**Mexico**

Mexico City   Oaxaca

## FRIDA KAHLO

Painter Frida Kahlo used bold colors to recreate her experience growing up in the bustling capital, Mexico City. Even Frida's home, now a museum, is a work of art. It's called La Casa Azul, or the Blue House, for its striking cobalt blue exterior.

## XÓCHITL GUADALUPE CRUZ LÓPEZ

In the Chiapas highlands, seven-year-old Xóchitl Guadalupe Cruz López helped her neighbors stay warm and protect their beloved trees by inventing a water heater that didn't need firewood to work.

## EUFROSINA CRUZ

In the southern city of Oaxaca, Eufrosina Cruz fights for the people who have lived in Mexico for centuries. Her work secured voting rights for Indigenous people.

# UNITED STATES

Each region of the United States is distinct. There are sprawling plains in the middle of the country, rugged mountains in the west, deserts in the southwest, and windswept coastlines in the northeast. The history of women in the US is just as varied and rich as its terrain. Here are some women who have been the changemakers during some of the most crucial moments in the country's history.

Alaska (U.S.)

Seattle

Pacific Ocean

Chicago

United States

New York

San Francisco

Washington, DC

Los Angeles

Atlanta

Atlantic Ocean

Hawaii (U.S.)

Puerto Rico (US)

## HARRIET TUBMAN

During the US Civil War, which threatened to permanently divide the North and the South, Harriet Tubman helped rescue enslaved people through a network known as the Underground Railroad.

## GRACE HOPPER

During World War II, computer programmer Grace Hopper decoded secret messages from other countries for the military.

## GLORIA STEINEM

In the 1970s, journalist Gloria Steinem was a key player in the feminist movement.

# SOUTH AMERICA

South America is one of the most biologically diverse places in the world. It spans two hemispheres and four major climate zones. The Amazon rain forest alone is home to more than 3 million different species! It's no surprise that many Rebels found inspiration for their work in the wonders of their homeland. The Brazilian countryside appears often in Cora Coralina's verses. In Ecuador, Nemonte Nenquimo fought to protect the rain forest she called home from oil companies that threatened to destroy it. And Peru-born author Isabel Allende moved to the vibrant city of Santiago, Chile, when she was young. She drew from her childhood there to write many of her books.

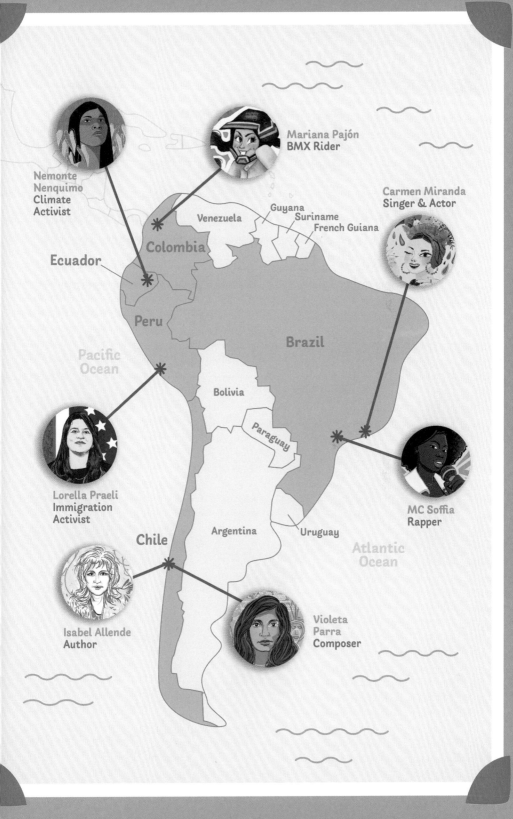

Nemonte
Nenquimo
Climate
Activist

Mariana Pajón
BMX Rider

Carmen Miranda
Singer & Actor

Venezuela

Guyana
Suriname
French Guiana

Colombia

Ecuador

Peru

Brazil

Pacific
Ocean

Bolivia

Paraguay

Lorella Praeli
Immigration
Activist

MC Soffia
Rapper

Chile

Argentina

Uruguay

Atlantic
Ocean

Isabel Allende
Author

Violeta
Parra
Composer

# BRAZIL

Brazil is full of color, from the green mountains of the highlands to the turquoise waters of the coast. The capital city of Rio de Janeiro hosts a massive, historic, and very colorful festival called Carnival every spring.

Brazil

Salvador

Brasília
★

Rio de Janeiro

São Paulo

Atlantic Ocean

## CARMEN MIRANDA

Though singer and dancer Carmen Miranda was born in Portugal, she grew up in Brazil and made a name for herself as a samba superstar.

## MARTA VIEIRA DA SILVA

Many talented soccer players come from Brazil, including Marta Vieira da Silva, who is widely considered to be the best female soccer player in history.

## MAYA GABEIRA

Another incredible athlete, big-wave surfer Maya Gabeira got her start on the beaches of Rio de Janeiro.

# SPOTLIGHT ON:

# COLOMBIA

This region won its independence from Spain in 1819, but it wasn't until 1903 that the country really resembled the Colombia seen on the map today. From the high-altitude, cyclist-friendly city of Bogotá to the coastlines on both the Caribbean Sea and the Pacific Ocean, Colombia is a land of extremes. It's also home to the largest tropical rain forest national park in the world.

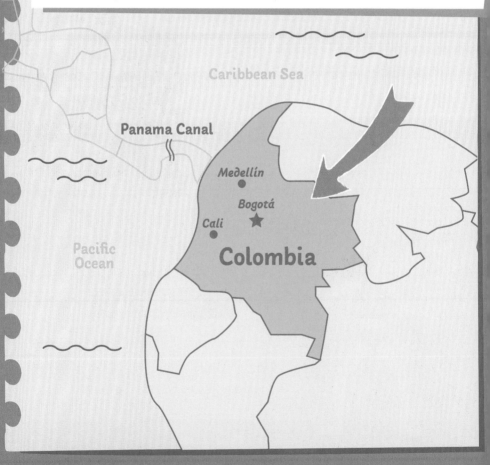

Caribbean Sea

Panama Canal

Medellín

Bogotá

Cali

Pacific Ocean

Colombia

## POLICARPA SALAVARRIETA

In the early 1800s, Policarpa Salavarrieta worked undercover in the city of Bogotá as a seamstress, gaining information about Spanish royalists' plans to take over the country.

## MARIANA PAJÓN

Growing up in Medellín in the 1990s, Mariana Pajón didn't feel safe at times, but she focused on her true love: BMX riding. She is now one of the most successful riders in the sport.

## MARÍA ISABEL URRUTIA

In 2000, super-strong weightlifter María Isabel Urrutia became the first-ever Colombian to win an Olympic gold medal.

# EUROPE

Evidence of ancient civilizations can still be found all over Europe today. The Colosseum in Rome is the world's largest amphitheater. In Greece, visitors can tour the remains of ancient Athens's prominent buildings at the Acropolis. Through Europe's long history, women have led countries, created timeless art, and fought for equality. In ancient Britain, Queen Boudicca fought against the Romans. During the 1500s, Queen Elizabeth I's intelligence and strategic thinking led the United Kingdom into a golden age of unity and progress. And in France, Pauline Léon fought for women's rights during the French Revolution and encouraged other women to speak up too.

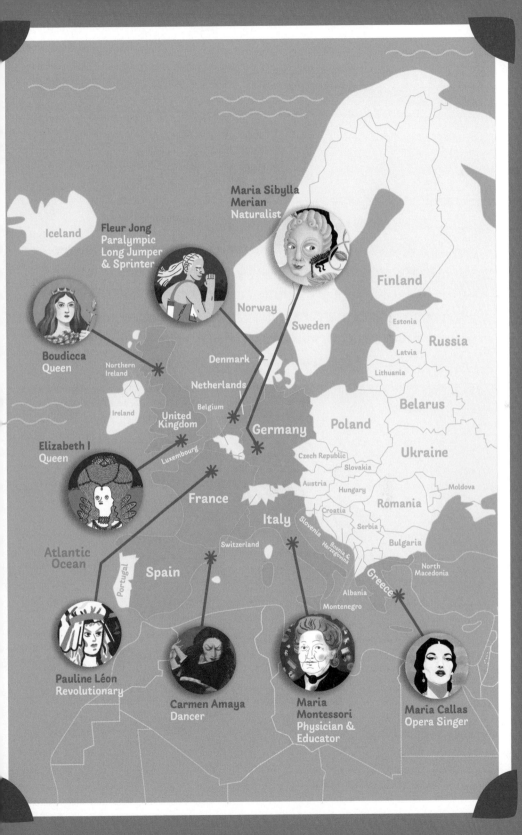

Iceland

Maria Sibylla
Merian
Naturalist

Fleur Jong
Paralympic
Long Jumper
& Sprinter

Finland

Norway

Sweden

Estonia

Russia

Boudicca
Queen

Northern
Ireland

Denmark

Latvia

Lithuania

Ireland

Netherlands

Belgium

United
Kingdom

Germany

Belarus

Poland

Elizabeth I
Queen

Luxembourg

Czech Republic

Ukraine

Slovakia

France

Austria

Hungary

Moldova

Italy

Croatia

Slovenia

Romania

Serbia

Bulgaria

Atlantic
Ocean

Switzerland

Bosnia &
Herzegovina

Greece

North
Macedonia

Portugal

Spain

Albania

Montenegro

Pauline Léon
Revolutionary

Carmen Amaya
Dancer

Maria
Montessori
Physician &
Educator

Maria Callas
Opera Singer

# ITALY

Surrounded by the sea and shaped like a boot, Italy is a long peninsula. On the Amalfi Coast, colorful towns nestle into cliffs overlooking the sea. Tuscany is known for its rolling green hills, and in Venice, people travel along the city's canals in special boats called gondolas. From meals to museums, there is always something for people to marvel at in Italy.

## ARTEMISIA GENTILESCHI

Artist Artemisia Gentileschi was known for using dark, rich colors for her moody portraits. She was the first female student at the Florence Academy of Fine Art.

## GAE AULENTI

Gae Aulenti is regarded as one of the greatest architects in history. In addition to transforming buildings into stunning museum spaces, she designed furniture, lamps, and other decorative items.

## LINA BO BARDI

Also an architect, Lina Bo Bardi focused on dreaming up incredible buildings. One of her most famous designs is called the Glass House. It's an all-glass box suspended over a forest—it looks like a modern tree house!

# SPOTLIGHT ON:

# POLAND

Poland sits at the heart of Europe. There are beaches along the Baltic Sea, and dense forests cover one-third of the country. Poland's central location has made it a prime target for conflict during periods of war and unrest. Many incredible women have persevered through Poland's stormy history and made a lasting impact in the world. For example, the first two women to earn Nobel Prizes were Polish.

Baltic Sea

Poland

Białystok

Warsaw

Łódź

Kraków

## MARIE CURIE

Scientist Marie Curie, born Maria Skłodowska, discovered two radioactive metals: polonium and radium.
Her work led to the development of an important cancer treatment.

## MARIA GOEPPERT MAYER

Maria Goeppert Mayer changed the field of nuclear physics by discovering the structure of atomic nuclei.

## IRENA SENDLEROWA

Humanitarian Irena Sendlerowa bravely made her mark on the world during World War II. She saved more than 2,500 Jewish children by giving them different names to keep them safe from the Nazis.

# ASIA

Asia is the largest continent in the world. It's made up of 48 countries. Nearly every climate can be found in Asia, from the frigid tundra of Siberia to the tropical warmth of Vietnam. Throughout history and all across this massive land, women have been leading, creating, and innovating. Seondeok of Silla was the first queen of Korea after a long line of kings. During her reign, the arts thrived. In modern-day Thailand, landscape architect Kotchakorn Voraakhom designs parks, buildings, and features that help sinking cities in flood-prone areas. Japanese inventor Yoky Matsuoka has invented special mechanical arms for people who have had strokes.

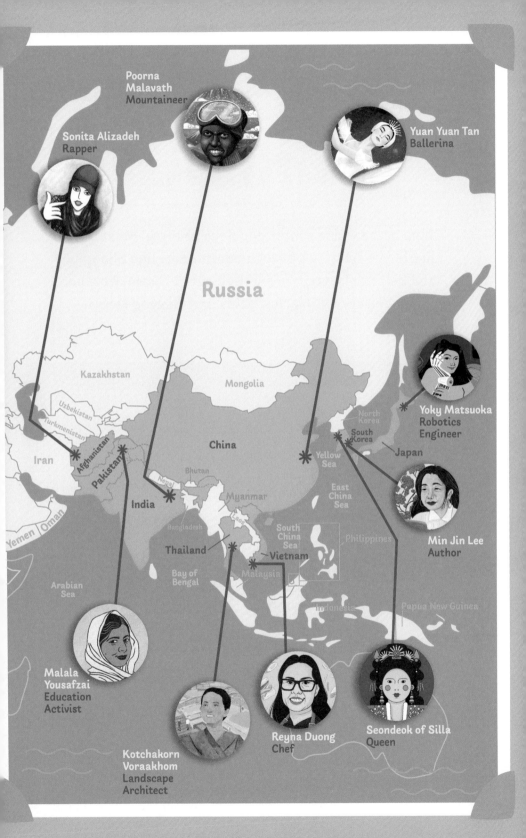

Sonita Alizadeh
Rapper

Poorna
Malavath
Mountaineer

Yuan Yuan Tan
Ballerina

Russia

Kazakhstan

Mongolia

Uzbekistan

Turkmenistan

Iran

Afghanistan

Pakistan

China

Bhutan

Nepal

India

Myanmar

Laos

Bangladesh

Thailand

Bay of
Bengal

South
China
Sea

Vietnam

Malaysia

Yellow
Sea

North
Korea

South
Korea

Japan

East
China
Sea

Philippines

Yoky Matsuoka
Robotics
Engineer

Min Jin Lee
Author

Yemen

Oman

Arabian
Sea

Indonesia

Papua New Guinea

Malala
Yousafzai
Education
Activist

Kotchakorn
Voraakhom
Landscape
Architect

Reyna Duong
Chef

Seondeok of Silla
Queen

# CHINA

China is the world's most populous country. Most people live in the country's busy, modern cities like Shanghai and Beijing. The rest are spread out in the countryside among sprawling rice fields and flowing rivers.

China

Beijing
Dandong
Chongqing
Shanghai
Hong Kong

## QIU JIN

In the 19th century, Qiu Jin refused to accept the unequal treatment of women in China. She spoke out for women's rights in the pages of the magazine she started and even trained other revolutionaries at a secret school.

## LUO DENGPING

In recent years, Luo Dengping's unique talent of scrambling up rock faces at incredible speeds earned her the nickname Spider-Woman!

## XIAN ZHANG

Xian Zhang fell in love with music as she grew up in the riverside city of Dandong. She went on to become an orchestra conductor.

# SPOTLIGHT ON:

# INDIA

India is a country steeped in unique customs and traditions. For instance, during the Hindu holiday Holi, cities and towns are flooded with people throwing colorful powders and creating rainbow clouds in the air. Many women in India have fought to preserve the things that make their home special.

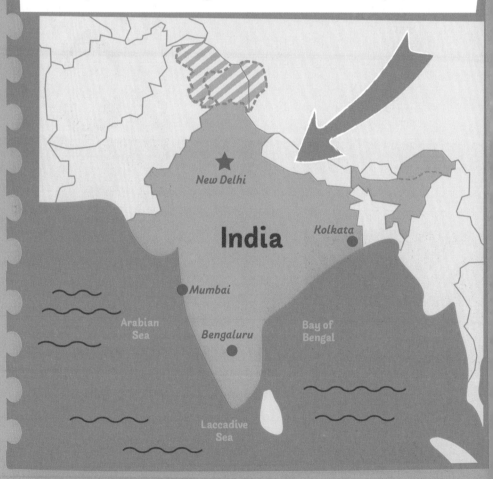

New Delhi

India

Kolkata

Mumbai

Arabian
Sea

Bengaluru

Bay of
Bengal

Laccadive
Sea

## LAKSHMI BAI

In the city of Jhansi, along the Pahuj River, Queen Lakshmi Bai created an army of both men and women to fight back against the British, who were trying to take control of her kingdom.

## PURNIMA DEVI BARMAN

Up north, among bright green tea fields, wildlife biologist Purnima Devi Barman works to save the hargila stork, an endangered bird found only in India.

## ASMA KHAN

Chef Asma Khan does her part to spread Indian traditions by teaching people the recipes she learned growing up in Kolkata (formerly known as Calcutta).

# AFRICA

The history of extraordinary women on the African continent is rich and varied. Long ago, Hatshepsut and Cleopatra ruled over Egypt. Later, Queen Yaa Asantewaa stood up to colonial soldiers in Ghana, and Empress Taytu Betul fought to keep her people free in Ethiopia. Artists, activists, and scientists have also thrived in Africa. From the bustling streets of the city of Johannesburg, South Africa, Miriam Makeba sang protest songs that were heard around the world. In a tropical city on the West African coast, Leymah Gbowee built a network of women committed to peace. And deep in a forest in East Africa, veterinarian Gladys Kalema-Zikusoka protects endangered mountain gorillas.

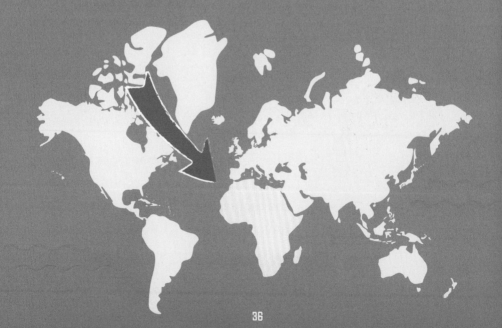

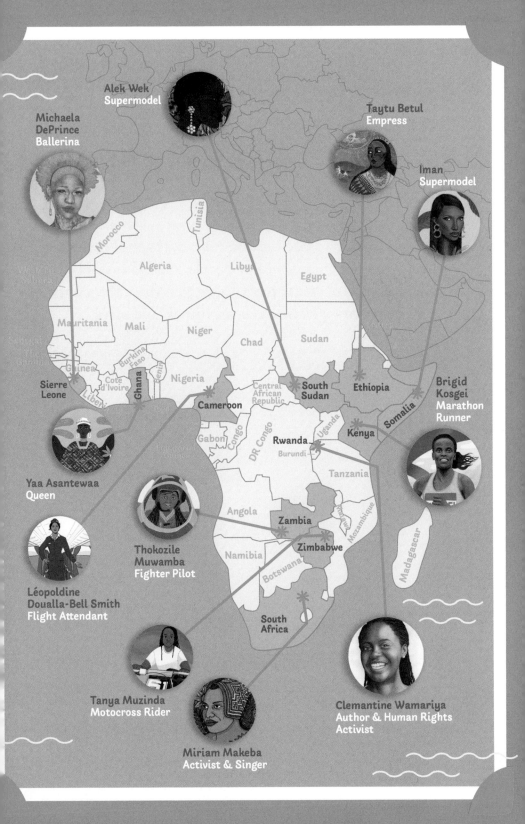

Alek Wek
**Supermodel**

Michaela
DePrince
**Ballerina**

Taytu Betul
**Empress**

Iman
**Supermodel**

Brigid
Kosgei
**Marathon
Runner**

Morocco

Tunisia

Algeria

Libya

Egypt

Mauritania

Mali

Niger

Chad

Sudan

Sierre
Leone

Guinea

Burkina
Faso

Benin

Côte
d'Ivoire

Ghana

Nigeria

Central
African
Republic

**South
Sudan**

Ethiopia

**Cameroon**

Gabon

Congo

DR Congo

**Rwanda**

Uganda

Burundi

**Kenya**

Somalia

Yaa Asantewaa
**Queen**

Thokozile
Muwamba
**Fighter Pilot**

Angola

Tanzania

Mozambique

Madagascar

**Zambia**

**Zimbabwe**

Léopoldine
Doualla-Bell Smith
**Flight Attendant**

Namibia

Botswana

Tanya Muzinda
**Motocross Rider**

**South
Africa**

Miriam Makeba
**Activist & Singer**

Clemantine Wamariya
**Author & Human Rights
Activist**

# KENYA

The landscape of Kenya includes vast savannas and acres of nature preserves. Nairobi, the capital city, is home to more than 4 million people. A large system of national parks protects the wildlife that roam the plains: elephants, giraffes, zebras, rhinos, and more.

Kenya

Kisumu

★ Nairobi

Indian Ocean

Mombasa

## WANGARI MAATHAI

To keep Kenya's environment healthy and thriving and to keep the women of Kenya safe and employed, Wangari Maathai started planting seedlings. More than 51 million trees have been planted as part of her Green Belt Movement.

## BRIGID KOSGEI

Olympic medalist Brigid Kosgei discovered her talent for long-distance running when she had to jog six miles every morning to get to school on time. On her way, she would see professional runners training. She vowed to be like them one day.

## LUPITA NYONG'O

Though she was born in Mexico, actor Lupita Nyong'o was raised in Kenya, mostly in the capital, Nairobi. She tells stories of climbing mango trees, eating lots of guava, and playing with her cousins in the town of Rata in western Kenya.

# NIGERIA

Nigeria lies in West Africa. There are rain forests and mangrove swamps in the south, mountains in the west, and vast savannas and plains. Nigeria is the most populous of all of the countries in Africa, and Lagos is its largest city.

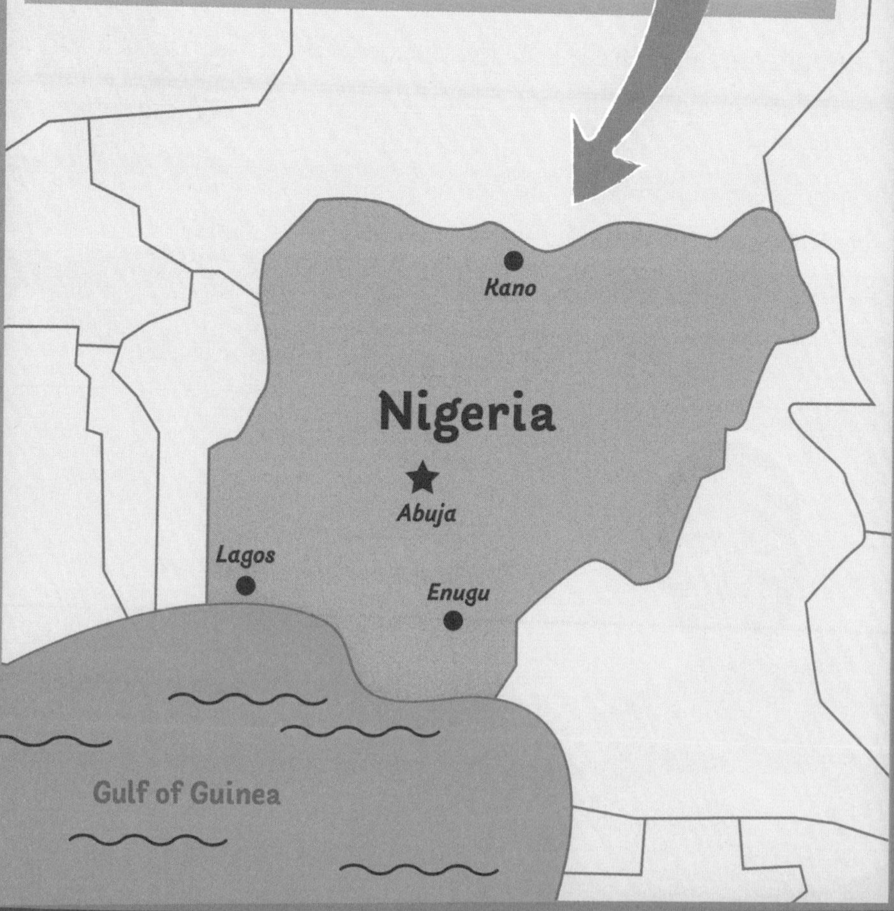

Kano

## Nigeria

★
Abuja

Lagos

Enugu

Gulf of Guinea

## SANDRA AGUEPOR-EKPERUOH

Sandra Aguepor-Ekperuoh defied expectations when she turned her love of tinkering into a career as a mechanic in Lagos. She didn't want other women to be held back by unreliable cars that might break down, so she dedicates her time to training other women to fix their own cars.

## CHIMAMANDA NGOZI ADICHIE

Chimamanda Ngozi Adichie was born in Enugu, in southern Nigeria. When she was 10 years old, she read the novel *Things Fall Apart* by Chinua Achebe, who was also from Nigeria. It opened her eyes and stimulated her creativity. She grew up to write novels that are set in her home country.

## LADI KWALI

Women in Nigeria have been making pottery forever. Ladi Kwali continued the ancient tradition. She mastered all sorts of techniques, from traditional ones to more modern ones, and shared her excellence with the whole world.

# OCEANIA

Oceania is made up entirely of islands scattered throughout the Central and South Pacific Ocean. Australia, Papua New Guinea, and New Zealand are the largest countries. Rebels from these nations have shown incredible determination and bravery. During World War II, New Zealand—born Nancy Wake served as a spy for British intelligence agencies. She was nicknamed "the White Mouse" because she was so clever and elusive. In 2010, Australian Jessica Watson became the youngest person to sail around the world alone. She hopped in her pink sailboat and was at sea for 210 days. At the Australia Zoo, conservationist Bindi Irwin works to protect animals big and small. Bindi and her family even live at the zoo among kangaroos and koalas.

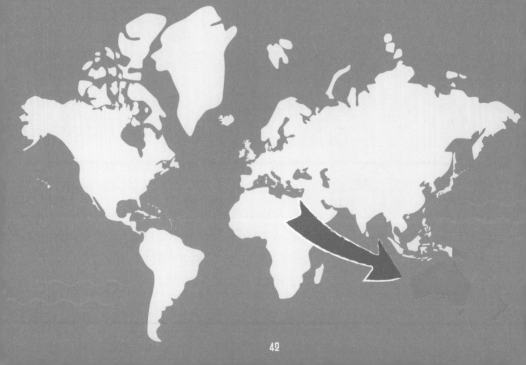

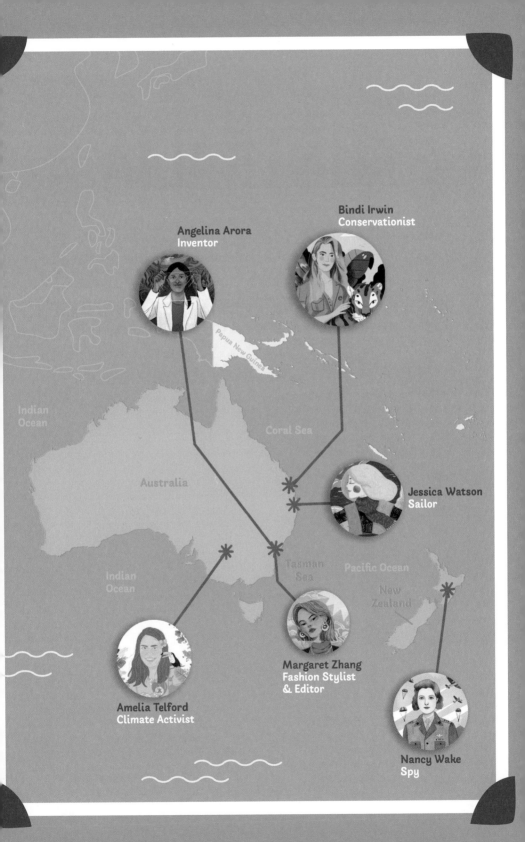

Angelina Arora
**Inventor**

Bindi Irwin
**Conservationist**

Jessica Watson
**Sailor**

Margaret Zhang
**Fashion Stylist
& Editor**

Amelia Telford
**Climate Activist**

Nancy Wake
**Spy**

Papua New Guinea

Indian
Ocean

Coral Sea

Australia

Indian
Ocean

Tasman
Sea

Pacific Ocean

New
Zealand

# AUSTRALIA

Australia is one of the largest countries on the planet. Its unique location in the middle of the ocean makes its climate one of a kind. Certain animals are native only to Australia, like the koala, kangaroo, and platypus. Australia has more than 500 national parks to protect its nature and wildlife.

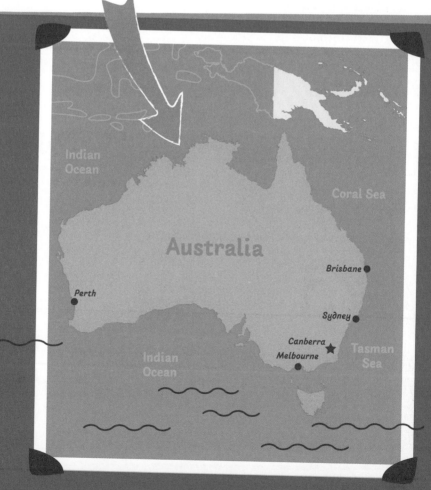

## AMELIA TELFORD

Indigenous climate activist Amelia Telford heads up an organization that empowers Indigenous people to get involved in climate justice and protect their land.

## ANGELINA ARORA

While still in high school, Angelina Arora decided to find a way to reduce plastic pollution. She developed a biodegradable material made from shrimp shells!

## MARGARET ZHANG

Sydney native Margaret Zhang found a career that combined three of her passions: art, fashion, and photography. She became the youngest editor in chief of *Vogue China*.

# REBEL GIRLS THROUGHOUT HISTORY

From Cleopatra to Amanda Gorman, women have accomplished amazing things in every time period in history. Travel through time and discover their contributions.

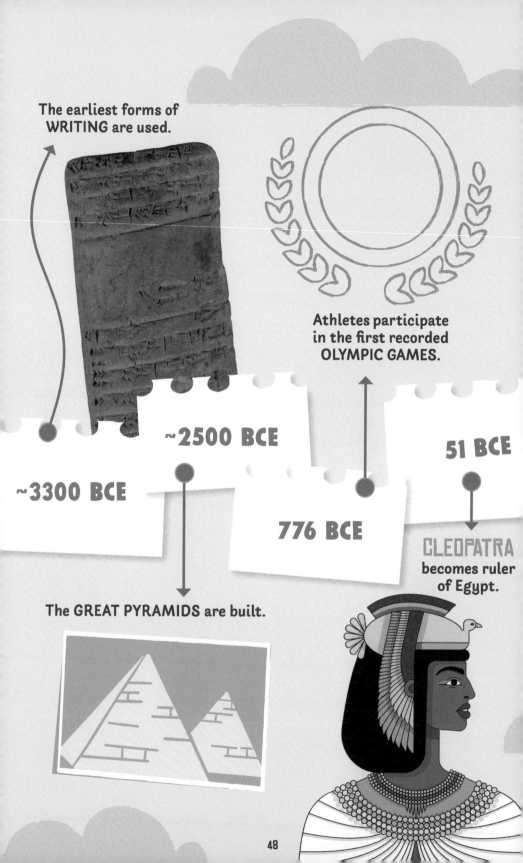

The earliest forms of WRITING are used.

Athletes participate in the first recorded OLYMPIC GAMES.

~2500 BCE

51 BCE

~3300 BCE

776 BCE

CLEOPATRA becomes ruler of Egypt.

The GREAT PYRAMIDS are built.

**HORTENSIA** delivers a speech in the Roman Forum.

**BOUDICCA** leads a revolt against the Roman Empire.

**~60 CE**

**632 CE**

**42 BCE**

**SEONDEOK OF SILLA** becomes the first female ruler of Korea.

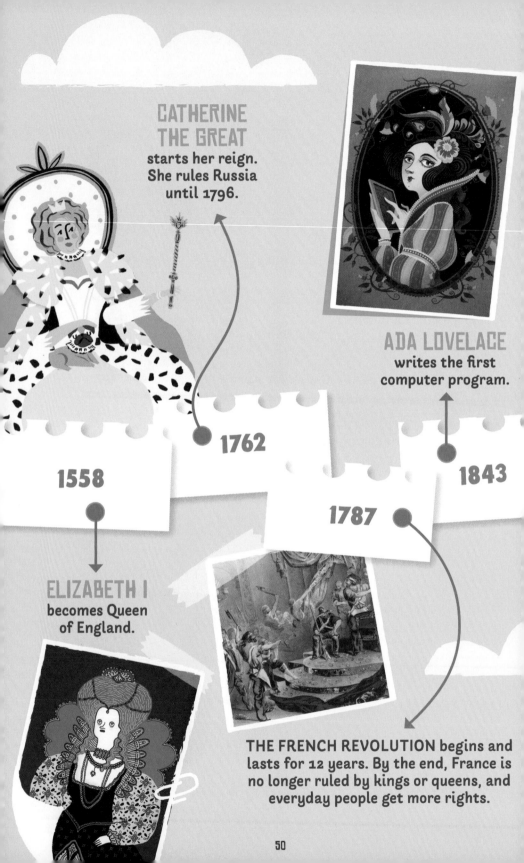

**CATHERINE THE GREAT** starts her reign. She rules Russia until 1796.

**ADA LOVELACE** writes the first computer program.

**1762**

**1558**

**1787**

**1843**

**ELIZABETH I** becomes Queen of England.

**THE FRENCH REVOLUTION** begins and lasts for 12 years. By the end, France is no longer ruled by kings or queens, and everyday people get more rights.

**HARRIET TUBMAN** escapes enslavement.

The US CIVIL WAR breaks out between the Union, or northern states, and the Confederacy, or southern states. It goes on for four years.

**1861**

**1898**

**1849**

**MARIE CURIE** discovers two new radioactive metals: polonium and radium.

## 1920

Women in the United States gain the RIGHT TO VOTE.

## 1914

WORLD WAR I begins. Fighting continues, mostly in Europe, but also in the Middle East and Africa, until 1918.

1910

1920

## 1917

The RUSSIAN REVOLUTION erupts. The country will never again be ruled by a powerful monarch called a tsar.

## 1926

JOSEPHINE BAKER

does her famous "banana dance" in Paris.

## 1939

**WORLD WAR II** erupts in Europe. Battles rage between the Axis and Allied powers until the war ends in 1945.

## 1932

**AMELIA EARHART** becomes the first woman to fly solo across the Atlantic Ocean.

## 1930

## 1929

After the crash of the stock market, the US suffers an economic crisis known as the **GREAT DEPRESSION.**

## 1938

**FRIDA KAHLO** has her first solo exhibition.

**1943**
**ALICIA ALONSO** dances the lead in the ballet *Giselle* for the first time.

**1940**
**ANDRÉE PEEL** joins the French Resistance.

**1950**

**1950**
THE KOREAN WAR starts. It lasts for three years.

**1941**
**HEDY LAMARR** co-invents the radio communications that will become the basis of Wi-Fi.

## 1955
### ROSA PARKS
refuses to give up her seat on a bus, setting off an important civil rights protest.

## 1963
### JANE GOODALL
publishes her cover story, "My Life Among the Wild Chimpanzees," in *National Geographic Magazine*.

## 1957
The Soviet Union launches the SPUTNIK satellite.

## 1960

## 1954
### THE VIETNAM WAR
begins when North Vietnamese forces invade South Vietnam. Later, US forces join the fighting. The war ends in 1975.

## 1960
### RUBY BRIDGES
becomes the first Black student to desegregate her elementary school in Louisiana.

## 1969
Astronauts WALK ON THE MOON for the first time.

**1973**

**BILLIE JEAN KING** plays a tennis match against a male opponent— and wins.

**1981**

**SANDRA DAY O'CONNOR** becomes the first woman to serve on the US Supreme Court.

**1970**

**1980**

**1977**

**WANGARI MAATHAI** starts the Green Belt Movement, which organizes women to plant trees throughout Kenya.

**1985**

**WILMA MANKILLER** becomes the first woman to serve as principal chief of the Cherokee Nation.

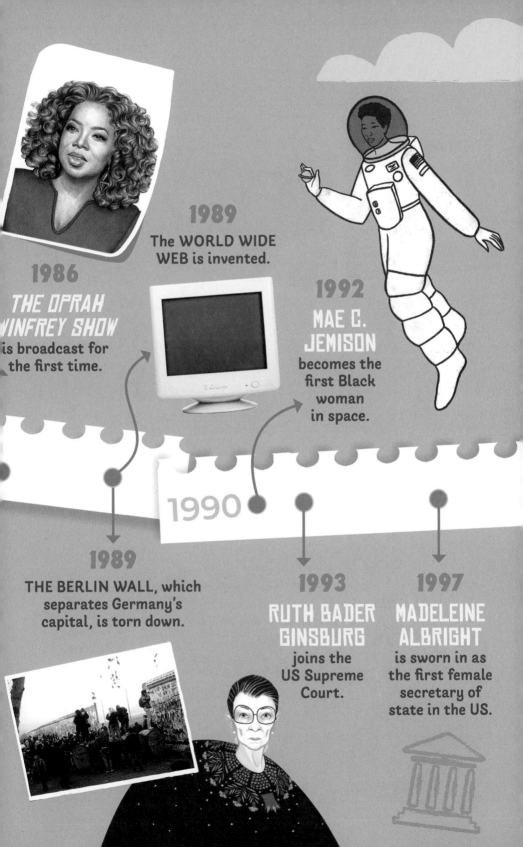

**1986**
*THE OPRAH WINFREY SHOW* is broadcast for the first time.

**1989**
The WORLD WIDE WEB is invented.

**1992**
*MAE C. JEMISON* becomes the first Black woman in space.

**1990**

**1989**
THE BERLIN WALL, which separates Germany's capital, is torn down.

**1993**
*RUTH BADER GINSBURG* joins the US Supreme Court.

**1997**
*MADELEINE ALBRIGHT* is sworn in as the first female secretary of state in the US.

**2017**

On Janury 21, more than 5 million people around the world participate in the **WOMEN'S MARCH.**

**2001**

**TEREZA LEE**
inspires the DREAM Act.

**2009**

**MICHELLE OBAMA**
becomes First Lady.

2010

**2014**

**MALALA YOUSAFZAI**
wins the Nobel Peace Prize.

2000

**2005**

**ANGELA MERKEL**
becomes the first female chancellor of Germany.

**2018**

**GRETA THUNBERG** starts her school strike.

**2021**

**SKY BROWN** becomes Great Britain's youngest Olympic medalist.

**2021**

**AMANDA GORMAN** delivers her poem "The Hill We Climb" at the US presidential inauguration.

**2020**

**2020**

**MAYA GABEIRA** breaks her own record in big-wave surfing.

**2020**

**KAMALA HARRIS** is nominated for US vice president. She is sworn in the next year.

UNITED STATES OF AMERICA
MAYA ANGELOU
E PLURIBUS UNUM
QUARTER DOLLAR

**2022**

**MAYA ANGELOU** is the first Black woman to appear on the US quarter.

# MEET THE REBELS

Learn facts about more than 300 amazing women and girls in the Rebel Girls universe. What are their likes, dislikes, fears, and dreams? They might be just like yours!

# ADA LOVELACE

## MATHEMATICIAN

December 10, 1815–November 27, 1852
United Kingdom

**Ada Lovelace's predictions and calculations made her the world's first computer programmer.**

 **SUPERPOWERS** *CALCULATION, FORWARD THINKING*

 Ada's father was the famous poet Lord Byron. Ada's mother encouraged her to pursue math, in order to be different from her father.

 Ada was known as the Enchantress of Numbers.

 Her best friend while she was growing up was her cat, Puff.

 The contributions Ada made to computing were only recognized a century after she died.

 There is a programming language named Ada in her honor.

YOUr TUrN!

Ada was obsessed with flying. She created a book, *Flyology*, about her fantasies of using steam-powered machinery to fly. What do you think air travel will look like in 30 years? Design a futuristic flying machine. Could it travel through space and time?

# ADELAIDE HERRMANN

## — MAGICIAN —

August 11, 1853–February 19, 1932
United Kingdom and United States

Adelaide Herrmann was a performer known as the Queen of Magic. She delighted audiences with enchanting tricks into her 70s.

**⚡SUPERPOWERS** *ILLUSION, DARING*

★ Adelaide practiced activities like acrobatics, dance, and a new sport called trick cycling.

★ She met her husband Alexander Herrmann ("Herrmann the Great") when she volunteered at one of his magic shows. After they married, Adelaide joined Alexander's show as a dancer and a human cannonball.

★ One of her most well-known dances involved red silks, which she twirled to mimic fire.

★ As part of Adelaide's "Noah's Ark" routine, she would dress up her dogs to look like elephants, lions, zebras, and other animals.

# AGATHA CHRISTIE
## —— author ——

September 15, 1890–January 12, 1976
United Kingdom

The world's best-selling novelist, Agatha Christie wrote 66 detective novels in her lifetime.

## ⚡SUPERPOWER
### CREATING SUSPENSE

✦ Agatha found inspiration by traveling to new places. Several of her books, such as *Murder on the Orient Express* and *Death on the Nile*, take place in the Middle East.

✦ Only the Bible and Shakespeare have outsold her books.

✦ Using the pen name Mary Westmacott, Agatha wrote six romance novels.

✦ She once dedicated a book to her dog. The inscription read, "Dear Peter, Most Faithful of Friends and Dearest of Companions, a Dog in a Thousand."

# ALEK WEK

## FASHION MODEL

Born April 16, 1977
South Sudan, United Kingdom,
and United States

Alek Wek is the first African
model to appear on the cover of
the American magazine *Elle*.

⭐ Alek grew up with eight brothers and sisters in what is now South Sudan. They lived in a village with no electricity or running water.

⭐ The outbreak of a devastating civil war caused Alek and her family to move to England.

⭐ Alek has booked modeling jobs with some of the most famous fashion designers in the world.

⭐ When a doctor wanted to fix her slightly misshapen finger, she refused.

⭐ Shakespeare and Company in Paris, France, is one of her favorite bookstores. She believes fashion tells stories, just like literature does.

# ALEXA CANADY
## NEUROSURGEON
Born November 7, 1950
United States

Alexa Canady helps treat diseases and infections in children's brains. Most of her patients are 10 years old or younger.

 **SUPERPOWERS** *COMPASSION, HEALING PEOPLE*

★ Alexa was the first Black woman in the US to become a neurosurgeon.

★ She almost dropped out of college. But then she took an internship in medicine and instantly fell in love with it!

★ Alexa was the chief of neurosurgery at the Children's Hospital of Michigan for 14 years, from 1987 to 2001.

★ Engaging and developing strong relationships with her patients is important to her. She can often be found playing video games or laughing with the children she helps.

# ALFONSINA STRADA

## CYCLIST

March 16, 1891–
September 13, 1959
Italy

**Alfonsina Strada was the only woman to compete in the Giro d'Italia, one of cycling's three major races.**

## SUPERPOWERS *SPEED, DAREDEVIL MOVES*

✳ Alfonsina won her first cycling race when she was just 13 years old. Her prize was a pig!

✳ In 1911, she broke the speed record for women's cycling. Her record held for 26 years.

✳ She raced on a 44-pound bike. Professional cyclists today race on bikes that weigh around 17 pounds.

✳ Alfonsina's parents didn't approve of her cycling, because, at the time, it was considered an activity only for men. But Alfonsina's husband was supportive and even gave her a new bike as a wedding gift.

# ALICE BALL
## CHEMIST
July 24, 1892–
December 31, 1916
United States

**Alice Ball developed the first successful treatment for leprosy.**

## ⚡SUPERPOWER *LOGIC*

✳ Alice was the first Black person and first woman to graduate from the University of Hawaii with a master of science degree in chemistry.

✳ At just 23 years old, she became the University of Hawaii's first female chemistry teacher.

✳ The treatment for leprosy that she created was later called the Ball Method. It helped thousands of patients get treated for the disease.

✳ Alice didn't get recognition for her discovery until six years after she died.

✳ In 2022, Hawaii established February 28 as Alice Ball Day.

# ALICE GUY BLACHÉ
## — FILMMAKER —
### July 1, 1873–March 24, 1968
### France and United States

**Alice Guy Blaché was the first woman to direct a film. From 1896 to 1906, she was likely the only female filmmaker in the world.**

## ⚡SUPERPOWER *STORYTELLING*

* As a child, Alice traveled by boat from France to Chile with her mother. Along the way, she daydreamed about fairies and beasts. Later, she would create whimsical worlds in her films.

* One of her first movies was called *The Cabbage Fairy*. Only one minute long, the film shows a young woman in a cabbage patch, waving a wand as newborn babies pop right out of the cabbages. Some film historians believe this was the first movie ever to tell a story.

* Together with her husband, Alice started her own film company, Solax. She directed, produced, or supervised more than 1,000 movies!

* In 1905, Alice used a device called a chronophone to capture singers lip-synching to a prerecorded track. It's possible that this was the very first music video!

**YOUR TURN!**

Alice Guy Blaché mastered the art of telling a short story on film—even without words! What story could you act out in one minute? Get on your feet and practice telling your tale.

# ALICE MILLIAT
## rower
May 5, 1884–May 19, 1957
France

Alice Milliat was a rower and an advocate for women's sports. She founded the International Women's Sports Foundation.

**SUPERPOWERS** ATHLETICISM, LEADERSHIP

+ During Alice's time, women were not allowed to fully compete in the Olympics. So she organized the Women's Olympic Games between 1922 and 1934.

+ Seventy years after Alice's efforts, the International Olympic Committee finally allowed women to participate in all Olympic Games.

+ Alice enjoyed field hockey, swimming, and rowing.

+ On International Women's Day in March 2021, a colorful statue of Alice was unveiled in Paris.

# ALICIA ALONSO
## — BALLERINA —
### December 21, 1920–October 17, 2019
### Cuba

A world-renowned prima ballerina, Alicia Alonso kept audiences on their toes as she danced with visual impairments.

## SUPERPOWERS GRIT, Grace

- Alicia was 19 when she developed an eye condition and began losing her sight.

- She had three eye surgeries. While she was bedridden, she practiced the choreography for her dream role as the lead in *Giselle*, using her hands to mark out the movements.

- Alicia finally got to perform in *Giselle* for the American Ballet Theatre. She was asked to step in for another dancer, who was injured.

- Alicia started her own dance company, which eventually became the Ballet Nacional de Cuba. Years later, her daughter Laura joined the company as a dancer.

# ALLYSON FELIX

## Sprinter

Born November 18, 1985
United States

Allyson Felix is the most decorated track-and-field athlete in US history.

**⚡SUPERPOWER SPEED**

* As part of her training, Allyson visualizes herself taking the steps she needs to run a great race.

* During the 2021 Olympic Games in Tokyo, some people didn't expect her to be at the top of her game because she was 35 years old and the mother of a young child. She won a gold medal and a bronze.

* By 2021, Allyson had won seven Olympic gold medals, three silver, and one bronze.

* She has her own sneaker company called Saysh.

* Allyson loves to Hula-Hoop and considers herself an expert!

# ALY RAISMAN
## GYMNAST & TEAM CAPTAIN
### Born May 25, 1994
### United States

As a member of the US women's gymnastics team, Aly Raisman won six Olympic medals.

## ⚡SUPERPOWER *Fierceness*

✳ Aly began gymnastics at a "mommy and me" class. She was just two years old.

✳ She was captain of the US women's gymnastics team in 2012 and 2016. In 2012, the team was dubbed the Fierce Five, and in 2016, they were called the Final Five.

✳ Aly has been a strong advocate for protecting female athletes.

✳ Aly's teammates, including Simone Biles and Gabby Douglas, sometimes jokingly refer to her as "grandma."

# AMANDA GORMAN
## POET

Born March 7, 1998
United States

**Amanda Gorman first made headlines when she became the youngest poet to recite her work at a US presidential inauguration.**

+ As a kid, Amanda suffered from a speech impediment and overcame it by reading her poems out loud.

+ After delivering her poem "The Hill We Climb" at President Joe Biden's inauguration, she published it as a book. It became a best seller.

+ She has a twin sister named Gabrielle who is a filmmaker and activist.

+ Amanda is the first poet ever to be on the cover of *Vogue* magazine.

Amanda writes poetry as a way to inspire social change. What is an issue that concerns you? Write a poem about it to encourage others to take action.

# AMEENAH GURIB-FAKIM

## PRESIDENT & SCIENTIST

Born October 17, 1959
Mauritius

Ameenah Gurib-Fakim was the president of Mauritius for three years. She is also a biologist who explores the wonder of plants.

## SUPERPOWERS
### KNOWLEDGE OF PLANTS, LEADERSHIP

⭐ Ameenah was the first woman to be elected president of Mauritius. She was also the country's first Muslim leader.

⭐ She studied the baobab tree and discovered that its fruit contains more protein than human milk.

⭐ For her work as a scientist, Ameenah received the African Union Commission Award for Women in Science.

⭐ She has written more than 28 scientific books. Some of them are used as references in schools.

# AMELIA EARHART

## AVIATOR

### July 24, 1897–circa July 2, 1937
### United States

**Amelia Earhart was the first female pilot to fly solo nonstop across the Atlantic Ocean.**

## ⚡SUPERPOWER *Fearlessness*

★ Amelia was instrumental in creating an organization called The 99s—a networking, mentoring, and education group for female pilots.

★ She wrote about her adventures and interest in flying in three popular books.

★ Once, after successfully navigating across the Atlantic Ocean, Amelia landed her plane in a cow field in Northern Ireland—much to the surprise of the cows!

★ Amelia loved tomato juice.

★ She was the first woman to receive the Distinguished Flying Cross—a military honor for extraordinary pilots.

# AMELIA TELFORD

## ENVIRONMENTAL ACTIVIST

Born 1994
Australia

**Amelia Telford founded Australia's first Indigenous-led youth climate network.**

**SUPERPOWERS**  *PASSION, PERSEVERANCE*

✳ When Amelia was three years old, she sent a letter to the prime minister asking him to change the national anthem from "Advance Australia Fair" to "We Are One."

✳ Amelia is a member of the Bundjalung community. She grew up on the coast of New South Wales near sunny beaches and lush rain forests.

✳ Seeing the coastline of her hometown eroding inspired Amelia to get involved in climate justice.

✳ Most people call her Millie.

Just like Amelia, you're never too young to make your voice heard. Is there something you'd like to see change at your school or in your town? Maybe you think recess should be 10 minutes longer? Or maybe you'd like to organize a beach or park cleanup to keep your favorite spot pristine? Whatever it is, write a letter to the person in charge (your school principal, teacher, mayor). State your opinion and make your case.

# AMNA AL HADDAD
## WEIGHTLIFTER

Born October 21, 1989
United Arab Emirates

Amna Al Haddad's weightlifting career in the sport took off when the International Weightlifting Federation began allowing Muslim women to compete in a unitard.

## ⚡SUPERPOWERS
### PHYSICAL AND MENTAL STRENGTH

* Amna was the first hijab-wearing Arab woman to compete in weightlifting.

* Before becoming a weightlifter, she worked as a journalist.

* When she was a teen, Amna suffered from depression. She says weightlifting helped her better recognize her self-worth.

* In 2016, she became the first Emirati to receive the Rosalynn Carter Fellowship for Mental Health Journalism.

* Amna has a rescue cat named Baby.

# ANDREA JENKINS

## POLITICIAN & POET

Born May 10, 1961
United States

**Andrea Jenkins is a poet and the first openly transgender Black woman elected to public office in the United States.**

 Andrea has published several books of poetry, including *The T Is Not Silent*, to increase awareness and understanding about transgender people.

 She once said, "Art serves many purposes; it can heal, educate, entertain, and challenge."

* Andrea was featured on the cover of *Time* magazine, along with other women who ran for office in 2017 and 2018.

 She signs all of her emails with "Love, Andrea" because she wants to add a little more kindness to the world.

# ANDRÉE PEEL
## French resistance fighter

February 3, 1905–March 5, 2010
France and United Kingdom

A resistance fighter in France during World War II, Andrée Peel helped save many British and American soldiers.

**SUPERPOWERS** DEFIANCE, STEALTH

★ Andrée was running a beauty salon when the German army invaded France in 1940. Life in France changed completely, and Andrée wanted to help defeat the Nazis.

★ As part of her resistance work, she circulated a secret newspaper and supplied the American and British troops with information on the whereabouts of Nazi soldiers.

★ Andrée helped guide British pilots in the middle of the night to secret runways that were lit only by torches.

★ During the war, Andrée was called Agent Rose.

★ She lived to be 105 years old!

# ANGELA JAMES
## HOCKEY PLAYER
Born December 22, 1964
Canada

Angela James won four gold medals during her 10 years with the Canadian Women's Hockey Team.

**SUPERPOWER**
*AGILITY*

+ Angela played in a boys' league before she was kicked out. Some boys didn't like that the team's best player was a girl!

+ She was the first Black woman and first openly gay player to be inducted into the Hockey Hall of Fame.

+ In addition to ice hockey, she played roller hockey. Her nickname was Maradona, after the great Argentinian soccer player Diego Maradona.

+ There is an arena named after her in Toronto, Canada.

# ANGELINA ARORA

## INVENTOR

Birthdate unknown
Australia

To reduce plastic waste, Angelina Arora created a biodegradable material using a substance found in shrimp shells.

## ⚡SUPERPOWERS OBSERVATION, INGENUITY

✦ Angelina got her idea for an eco-friendly material at her local fish shop. She noticed that shrimp shells look a lot like plastic.

✦ She competed against 1,800 students from 81 countries at the Intel International Science and Engineering Fair. She placed fourth in the world.

✦ In 2019, Angelina won the Young Conservationist of the Year award from the Australian Geographic Society.

✦ An aspiring doctor, she hopes her invention can one day be used to package medical supplies.

# ANN MAKOSINSKI
## INVENTOR

Born October 3, 1997
Canada

**Ann Makosinski is best known for creating a flashlight powered by the heat of a person's hand.**

**⚡SUPERPOWER** *INNOVATION*

✦ As a child, Ann spent her time listening to opera, watching silent movies, and practicing the piano and the violin. She didn't watch TV.

✦ She won the Google Science Fair at 15 years old with her invention of a thermoelectric flashlight.

✦ Ann was inspired to make the flashlight when she met people living without electricity while visiting her mother's hometown in the Philippines.

✦ Ann also designed a mug that uses the heat of a drink to charge a cell phone!

BALANCE, DARING

# ANNA OLGA ALBERTINA BROWN

aerialist
April 21, 1858–
after 1919
Poland

Known as Miss La La, Anna Olga Albertina Brown was a biracial 19th-century circus aerialist.

* Anna performed in the circus for the first time when she was just nine years old.

* She was most known for her "iron jaw act," where she would dangle from a strap using her teeth and spin around high in the air!

* Beloved impressionist artist Edgar Degas captured Anna's grace and strength on canvas with his piece *Miss La La at the Cirque Fernando*.

* In 1888, Anna married a contortionist. She and her husband had three daughters who also became circus performers.

# ANNE HIDALGO
## POLITICIAN
### Born June 19, 1959
### Spain and France

Anne Hidalgo was elected as mayor of Paris in 2014. In her role as leader, she has made the city greener.

## ⚡SUPERPOWER *CONVICTION*

* Anne is the first female mayor of Paris.

* She grew up speaking both Spanish and French.

* Along with other female mayors who are fighting climate change, Anne launched an initiative called Women4Climate.

* She banned cars from certain streets in Paris and helped build bike lanes to decrease pollution.

* Her local bookstore puts new books in Anne's mailbox, because they know how much she loves to read.

# ARETHA FRANKLIN
## SINGER

March 25, 1942–August 16, 2018
United States

**Aretha Franklin's mighty voice earned her
the noble nickname the Queen of Soul.**

**⚡SUPERPOWERS** *CONFIDENCE, POWERHOUSE VOCALS*

 When her first piano teacher came to her house, Aretha hid instead of taking the lesson.

 Her female fans loved her song "Respect." It became a rallying cry during the civil rights movement.

 Aretha once stepped in for opera singer Luciano Pavarotti when he was too sick to perform (with less than a day's notice!).

 She was afraid of flying and avoided traveling by plane as much as she could.

 Aretha was the first woman inducted into the Rock & Roll Hall of Fame.

**Your Turn!**

Aretha's song "Respect" became an anthem for women everywhere. Can you write a song that celebrates girls? Think of an empowering word or phrase, match it to a tune, and then . . . sing!

# ARIANNA HUFFINGTON

## AUTHOR & CEO
### Born July 15, 1950
### Greece and United States

Arianna Huffington is an author and businesswoman who cofounded the *Huffington Post*. She then became the founder and CEO of Thrive Global.

## SUPERPOWERS *WRITING, CONFIDENCE*

+ Born in Greece, Arianna's birth name was Arianna Stassinopoulos.

+ When she moved to the United Kingdom to attend Cambridge University, she barely spoke English. She joined a debate organization on campus to help her with her English. She was such a talented debater that she became president of the group.

+ Arianna wrote her first book when she was 23 years old. Her second book was rejected 37 times before getting published!

+ She loves country music.

# ARLAN HAMILTON
## INVESTOR

Born October 30, 1980
United States

Arlan Hamilton aims to fund businesses created by women, people of color, and members of the LGBTQIA+ community.

✦ When Arlan first started her journey to becoming an investor, she did not have a home. She often slept on friends' couches or even on the airport floor.

✦ She is the only gay Black woman to build a venture capital firm from the ground up.

✦ The first time someone agreed to invest in her vision, Arlan jumped up and did a dance!

✦ She has invested in more than 130 companies.

# ARTEMISIA GENTILESCHI

## Painter

July 8, 1593–
June 14, 1653
Italy

---

**Artemisia Gentileschi was the first female student at the Florence Academy of Fine Art.**

**SUPERPOWER**
VIBRANT PAINTING

* Artemisia painted in the Baroque style—a style of art from the 17th century that contains lots of drama, extravagance, movement, and deep, rich colors.

* Together with her father, Artemisia painted 26 figures on the ceiling of the home of Queen Henrietta Maria. Twenty-five of them were female, to showcase the power of women.

* Artemisia was friends with the famous astronomer Galileo. They regularly wrote letters to each other.

* After she died, many people assumed her paintings were made by male artists. It took many years for artists and historians to finally celebrate her talent.

# ASHLEY FIOLEK
## motocross racer
### Born October 22, 1990
### United States

Ashley Fiolek is a motocross racer and stuntwoman. She is deaf and uses sign language to communicate.

**SUPERPOWERS** *FOCUS, FEARLESSNESS*

* Ashley relies on the changing vibrations of the motorbike's engine to know when to change gears.

* She won her first national competition with her hair dyed pink. She considers it good luck!

* She was the first deaf person to appear on the talk show *Conan*. Her father translated so she could communicate with host Conan O'Brien.

* Ashley says it is more difficult being a woman in motocross than it is being deaf.

# ASMA KHAN

## CHEF

Born circa July 1969
India and
United Kingdom

Asma Khan is a chef
and cookbook author.
She owns a restaurant
in London called
Darjeeling Express.

## ⚡SUPERPOWERS
### AMBITION, AROMATIC FLAVORS

⭐ Asma was the first British chef to be featured in her own episode of the series *Chef's Table*.

⭐ She trained as a lawyer. Asma began cooking after she moved to England and felt homesick. Cooking Indian food gave her comfort.

⭐ Her cousins lovingly called her Ratatouille after the Disney film.

⭐ She works with an all-female team at her restaurant.

⭐ Asma loves sweets and is especially fond of ice cream and jam.

# ASTRID LINDGREN
## author
November 14, 1907–January 28, 2002
Sweden

Astrid Lindgren is best known for creating the character Pippi Longstocking.

**SUPERPOWERS** *CREATIVITY, COMPASSION*

★ Astrid grew up on a farm with her parents, two sisters, one brother, and lots of farmhands—everyone pitched in to help on the farm.

★ Throughout World War II, Astrid was a censor. She read letters to and from other countries, as well as military mail, and crossed out any information that the military did not want to be read by their enemies.

★ She wrote 34 chapter books and 41 picture books. All together, her books have sold about 165 million copies and been translated into more than 100 languages!

★ In 1996, an asteroid was named in her honor. She later joked, "From now on, please call me Asteroid Lindgren."

# AUDRE LORDE

## POET

February 18, 1934–November 17, 1992
United States

A feminist writer, Audre Lorde used her life work to confront racism, sexism, and homophobia.

+ Audre's name was originally spelled "Audrey," but she dropped the "Y" because she thought it looked better next to her last name.

+ When she was 17, Audre wrote a poem that was rejected by the school newspaper. So she submitted it to *Seventeen* magazine and became a published writer before starting college!

+ She described herself as "Black, feminist, lesbian, mother, warrior, poet."

+ Audre did an African naming ceremony before her death and took the name Gamba Adisa, which means "Warrior: She Who Makes Her Meaning Clear."

# AUDREY HEPBURN
## ACTOR &
## HUMANITARIAN

May 4, 1929–
January 20, 1993
Belgium, the Netherlands,
and United Kingdom

Audrey Hepburn was a film and
fashion icon who consistently
used her platform to give back.

## ⚡SUPERPOWERS CHARM, CHARITY

- When Audrey went hungry
  during World War II, she ate
  tulip bulbs in order to survive.
  Decades later, a breed of tulip was
  named after her.

- She once broke several bones in her back
  while filming a horseback riding scene in
  a movie.

- For her performance in the 1953 film *Roman
  Holiday*, Audrey won the Academy Award for
  best actress.

- She had a pet deer named Pippin!

- Her favorite color was cyan, a bluish-green.

# AUTUMN PELTIER
## CLEAN WATER ACTIVIST

Born September 27, 2004
Canada

Autumn Peltier fights for the First Nations communities to have access to clean drinking water.

## SUPERPOWER *Bravery*

* Autumn is Anishinaabe and is a member of the Wiikwemkoong First Nation.

* In 2018, she captivated audiences with a powerful speech at the United Nations World Water Day.

* She says her water warrior spirit comes from her great-aunt, Josephine Mandamin, who walked the shoreline of all five Great Lakes—a distance of more than 10,500 miles!

* Autumn takes her Bengal cat, Achilles, for walks outside.

# AVA DUVERNAY
## FILMMAKER
### Born August 24, 1972
### United States

Ava DuVernay addresses social injustice in her films and TV shows. Her work includes the series *When They See Us*, the documentary *13th*, and the long-running show *Scandal*.

* Ava is the first Black woman to win the award for best director at the Sundance Film Festival.

* In college, she studied to be a journalist. She didn't start making films until she was 32 years old.

* Ava directed *A Wrinkle in Time*, based on the beloved children's book by Madeleine L'Engle.

* She was the first Black woman to direct a film with a budget of $100 million.

* One of her favorite superheroes is a powerful female warrior named Big Barda.

**SUPERPOWER TENACITY**

# BANA ALABED
## ACTIVIST

Born June 7, 2009
Syria and Turkey

Bana Alabed grabbed the world's attention when, at seven years old, she tweeted about military attacks in her hometown of Aleppo, Syria.

### ⚡SUPERPOWER *courage*

✳ *Bana* is the name of a tall, bushy tree with light green leaves that grows in Syria.

✳ When she grows up, Bana wants to be a teacher like her mom.

✳ She has written two books, called *My Name Is Bana* and *Dear World: A Syrian Girl's Story of War and Plea for Peace*.

✳ Bana loves the Harry Potter book series.

✳ She often talks about the importance of literacy and education for all children.

# BARBARA HILLARY

## nurse & adventurer

June 12, 1931–November 23, 2019
United States

At 75 years old, Barbara Hillary became the first Black woman on record to reach the North Pole. Four years later, she trekked to the South Pole.

✦ Barbara was a nurse for 55 years. After she retired, she decided to go on adventures.

✦ She saw an ad that read, "See polar bears in their natural habitat." So she flew to Manitoba, Canada, and photographed humongous polar bears.

✦ The first time she tried dogsledding, her sled hit a rock. She flew through the air and was injured when she landed. She came home on crutches, but was determined to keep exploring snowy northern places.

✦ Barbara made sure to bring a lot of milk chocolate, her favorite, with her when she went to the South Pole.

# BEATRICE VIO
## fencer
Born March 4, 1997
Italy

Beatrice Vio, known as Bebe, is an Italian wheelchair fencer. She contracted meningitis as a child, and doctors had to amputate her forearms and her legs below the knees.

**SUPERPOWER** *TOUGHNESS*

- The only fencer in the world without arms and legs, Bebe invented a fencing technique that would work for her.

- She won the World Cup in Canada, the European Championships in Italy, the World Championship in Hungary, and the gold medal at the Paralympics in Rio de Janeiro.

- Bebe saw fencers in a gym when she was five years old. She said it was "love at first sight!"

- When she was younger, she wanted to open a clothing store for babies.

# BEATRIX POTTER

## author & illustrator

July 28, 1866–December 22, 1943
United Kingdom

**Beatrix Potter became famous for her beloved book
*The Tale of Peter Rabbit*.**

**SUPERPOWER** *IMAGINATION*

✳ Beatrix named her book after her own pet rabbit named Peter Piper.

✳ *The Tale of Peter Rabbit* originally had black-and-white illustrations, and it was turned down by publishers. Beatrix redid her illustrations in color, and the book became a big success.

✳ Beatrix is actually her middle name. Her first name is Helen.

✳ She kept a secret diary written in code. It was cracked by a fan of hers more than 20 years after she died!

✳ Beatrix bred the Herdwick sheep and helped save it from extinction.

Beatrix wrote and illustrated stories about the animals she encountered. What animals live with you or in your neighborhood? Draw and make up your own short story about them.

# BESSIE COLEMAN

## PILOT

January 26, 1892–April 30, 1926
United States

Bessie Coleman was the first Black woman and first Native American to earn a pilot's license.

## SUPERPOWER aerial STUNTS

* Bessie learned French to earn her international pilot's license.

* While living in Chicago, she ran a popular chili shop.

* For her wild stunt shows, she was known as Queen Bess or Brave Bessie.

* Bessie performed aerial acrobatics, including flying upside down, drawing figure eights in the sky, and making loops with her plane. When she wasn't the pilot, she'd walk on the wings and parachute down to the ground.

# BESSIE STRINGFIELD

## MOTORCYCLIST
1911–February 16, 1993
United States

Bessie Stringfield was the first Black woman to ride across every state in the continental United States.

**SUPERPOWERS** *GUTS, INDEPENDENCE*

* Bessie would perform the "wall of death" stunt, where she raced around in a metal globe.

* She was a motorcycle dispatch rider during World War II.

* Bessie used to compete in motorcycle races disguised as a man.

* She had only one accident in her whole life—when she was 64 years old!

* She taught at least two of her husbands how to ride motorcycles.

# BEYONCÉ
## SINGER, SONGWRITER, & BUSINESSWOMAN
### Born September 4, 1981
### United States

**A powerhouse singer and songwriter, Beyoncé became famous while performing with the girl group Destiny's Child before going solo.**

* In order to overcome stage fright, Beyoncé adopted the alter ego "Sasha Fierce" for her performances.

* She has the record for the most Grammy wins by a woman.

* She is allergic to perfume. Her own fragrances have added chemicals that allow her to wear them.

* In 2012, a species of fly was named after her, the *Scaptia beyonceae*.

* She likes jalapeños on her pizza.

**⚡SUPERPOWERS** *STAGE PRESENCE, POWERFUL LYRICS*

# BILLIE JEAN KING

## TENNIS PLAYER

Born November 22, 1943
United States

Billie Jean King led the fight for equal pay for men and women in tennis. In 1973, she won the "Battle of the Sexes" tennis match against a male player.

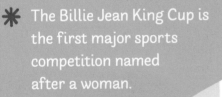

## SUPERPOWERS  *SPIRIT, SWIFTNESS*

 Billie was awarded the Presidential Medal of Freedom in 2009. She was the first female athlete to receive the award.

 Her favorite color is purple.

* She is one of the first openly gay athletes in the US and consistently speaks out for the LGBTQIA+ community.

* The Billie Jean King Cup is the first major sports competition named after a woman.

# BINDI IRWIN
## CONSERVATIONIST

Born July 24, 1998
Australia

Dedicated to protecting wildlife, Bindi Irwin works as a zookeeper at the Australia Zoo, owned by her family.

**SUPERPOWER**
*KINDNESS*

* Bindi's father, the late TV personality Steve Irwin, named her after one of his favorite crocodiles at the zoo!

* When she was nine, Bindi began hosting her own show called *Bindi the Jungle Girl*.

* Bindi won *Dancing with the Stars* and donated all her award money to conservation efforts.

* She named her daughter Grace Warrior after her grandmother Grace and her father, who was an amazing "wildlife warrior."

# BONNIE CHIU
## SOCIAL ENTREPRENEUR
Born November 3, 1992
Hong Kong and United Kingdom

Bonnie Chiu founded a project to empower girls and women by teaching them how to express themselves through photography.

* When Bonnie learned that two-thirds of people in the world who cannot read are women, she started her photography training program, called Lensational.

* Her program has provided training in many countries, including Pakistan, Bangladesh, the Philippines, and Indonesia.

* She loves paddleboarding and says she can't live without rice.

* Her favorite color is yellow.

SUPERPOWER
OUTSIDE-THE-BOX THINKING

# BOUDICCA
## QUEEN
### Circa 33-61 CE
### United Kingdom

The queen of the ancient British Iceni tribe, Boudicca led a revolt against the Roman Empire in the year 60.

**⚡SUPERPOWER** *LEADERSHIP*

- According to legend, Boudicca led an attack against the Romans after her daughters were tortured by them.

- She has inspired many powerful women throughout history, including Queen Elizabeth I and Queen Victoria.

- There is a statue of her near Westminster Bridge in London.

- Her name means "victory" in Celtic.

# BRENDA CHAPMAN
## — DIRECTOR —

Born November 1, 1962
United States

Brenda Chapman was the first
woman to direct an animated film
for a major studio.

## ⚡SUPERPOWERS
### Bravery, Storytelling

+ Brenda wrote and co-directed
the Disney film *Brave*, which was
inspired by her relationship with
her daughter.

+ Brenda has always loved fairy tale
movies. Her favorites are *Beauty
and the Beast* and *The Little
Mermaid*.

+ She has worked on many famous
animated films, including *The Lion
King*, *Cars*, and *Up*.

+ She was the first woman to win
an Academy Award for best
animated feature.

# BRENDA MILNER

## NEUROPSYCHOLOGIST

Born July 15, 1918
United Kingdom and Canada

**Brenda Milner pioneered many studies of the brain and memory.**

* Brenda made the groundbreaking discovery that the brain has at least two different memory systems: one for motor skills (things that involve specific movements, like jumping or writing) and the other for names, faces, and experiences.

* When Brenda was six years old, she and her mother contracted a dangerous flu! Fortunately, they both recovered.

* Brenda's father taught her German from a young age. This later inspired her research on how second languages affect the brain.

* Even after turning 100, Brenda continues to work and study!

# BRIGETTE LACQUETTE

## ICE HOCKEY PLAYER

Born November 10, 1992
Canada

**Brigette Lacquette is the first First Nations player for the Canadian women's Olympic hockey team.**

**SUPERPOWER**
**SWIFTNESS**

* Brigette's hockey stick was exhibited in the Hockey Hall of Fame.

* Growing up, Brigette would skate every winter on an outdoor rink her father built outside their home.

* Her dogs are named Fin and Zig.

* Brigette loves playing all sports, including volleyball and golf.

* In 2021, she became the first Indigenous woman to scout for a National Hockey League team.

# BRIGID KOSGEI

## Marathon runner

Born February 20, 1994
Kenya

Brigid Kosgei holds the women's world record for running a marathon in 2 hours and 14 minutes.

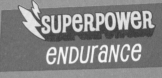

**SUPERPOWER**
ENDURANCE

- Brigid discovered her talent for running when she had to jog six miles every day to get to school on time.

- She won the silver medal in marathon running at the 2020 Summer Olympics in Tokyo.

- Before she broke the world record, the previous record was held for 16 years.

- Brigid's favorite dish is vegetables with *ugali*, a regional African cornmeal porridge cake.

# BUFFALO CALF ROAD WOMAN
## — warrior —

Circa 1850s–1879
United States

Buffalo Calf Road Woman was a brave Cheyenne warrior who rode into a hail of bullets to save her brother during a battle.

## ⚡SUPERPOWERS
### HORSEBACK RIDING, HEROISM

★ Because of Buffalo Calf Road Woman's act of bravery during the Battle of Rosebud, the Cheyenne refer to that day as the Battle Where the Girl Saved Her Brother.

★ She was also known as Buffalo Calf Robe, Buffalo Calf Trail Woman, and Brave Woman.

★ She was the only woman to fight in the Battle of Little Bighorn.

★ In 2005, a Cheyenne elder revealed to a newspaper that chiefs asked the tribe to keep a vow of silence about the Battle of Little Bighorn for 100 summers.

# CARMEN AMAYA

## Dancer

Circa 1918–
November 19, 1963
Spain

**A Romani-Spanish performer, Carmen Amaya was one of the most famous and influential flamenco dancers.**

## ⚡SUPERPOWERS Drama, Footwork

★ Carmen's father and aunt taught her to dance. She never received any formal training.

★ She said her dancing was inspired by the sea and the way the waves moved.

★ Sometimes she wore flamenco dresses, but Carmen preferred to dress in a matador costume of pants and a bolero jacket.

★ Famous conductor Arturo Toscanini said Carmen had the "charisma of a rock star. Her lightning footwork, faster than the eye could comprehend, made audiences dizzy."

# CARMEN HERRERA

## ARTIST

May 30, 1915–February 12, 2022
Cuba and United States

**Carmen Herrera was a Cuban American abstract painter who achieved worldwide fame late in her career.**

## ⚡SUPERPOWERS

### ABSTRACT PAINTING, GEOMETRY

★ Carmen first became famous for her paintings at the age of 89.

✦ She was passionate about creating straight lines in her works, because for her, they were "the beginning of all structures."

★ Carmen planned out her paintings using mathematical calculations.

✦ She also enjoyed woodworking. Her favorite type of wood was mahogany.

# CARMEN MIRANDA

## SINGER & ACTOR

February 9, 1909–August 5, 1955
Portugal, Brazil,
and United States

After appearing in Hollywood films, Carmen Miranda became known for wearing colorful clothing and elaborate headdresses.

**SUPERPOWERS** *CHARISMA, COSTUME MAKING*

+ Carmen was born in Portugal. But after moving to Brazil with her family when she was a baby, Carmen never returned to her birth country.

+ She was quite small and wore very high heels to appear taller while performing.

+ Carmen helped popularize Brazilian samba in the United States.

+ Her image was the inspiration for the logo of a brand of bananas.

# CATHERINE THE GREAT
## empress
May 2, 1729–November 17, 1796
Russia

Catherine the Great was the empress of Russia. She ruled for more than 30 years—the longest reign of any leader in the country's history.

**SUPERPOWER** *STRATEGIC THINKING*

 Catherine was born in Prussia (modern-day Germany) as Sophie von Anhalt-Zerbst.

✦ She wrote fairy tales and operas.

✦ Catherine loved art and amassed an enormous collection. She founded the State Hermitage Museum in St. Petersburg, Russia—the largest art museum in the world.

✦ She started Russia's first school for women, the Smolny Institute.

# CELIA CRUZ
## SINGER

October 21, 1925–
July 16, 2003
Cuba and United States

---

**Known as the Queen of Salsa, singer Celia Cruz helped make salsa music popular in the United States.**

* Celia's career lasted 60 years. She recorded more than 80 albums and won a Recording Academy Lifetime Achievement Award.

* Onstage, she loved to wear colorful wigs and sparkly costumes.

* Although Celia is known for salsa music, she also performed reggaeton and rumba.

* Whenever she was on stage, she would cry out, *Azucar!* (Sugar!)

* Celia originally wanted to be a teacher.

## SUPERPOWERS
ENERGY, ENCHANTING VOICE

# CHARLOTTE WORTHINGTON

## BMX CYCLIST

Born June 26, 1996
United Kingdom

**Charlotte Worthington is the first woman to win an Olympic gold medal in freestyle BMX.**

## SUPERPOWERS
### DETERMINATION, STUNT RIDING

* Charlotte rode stunt scooters for about eight years before taking up cycling.

* Before going professional as a cyclist, she worked as a chef.

* Charlotte landed the first 360 backflip in a woman's competition.

* She enjoys Italian food. But she is not a fan of raw tomatoes.

# CHIMAMANDA NGOZI ADICHIE

## author

Born September 15, 1977
Nigeria

Chimamanda Ngozi Adichie's stories about Nigeria, migration, gender, and war have influenced readers around the world.

* Chimamanda dropped out of medical school to pursue writing.

* She did a TED Talk called "We Should All Be Feminists." Beyoncé used a sample of the talk in her song "Flawless."

* Chimamanda says chocolate is essential to her writing process.

* Her writing has been translated into more than 30 languages.

## SUPERPOWERS
### HONESTY, STORYTELLING

# CHLOE KIM
## SNOWBOARDER
### Born April 23, 2000
### United States

Chloe Kim is the youngest athlete to medal at the X Games and the first woman to win two Olympic gold medals in the snowboard halfpipe.

## ⚡SUPERPOWERS *BALANCE, OPTIMISM*

❇ Chloe's dog, Reese, posed with her on the cover of *Sports Illustrated*.

❇ To calm her nerves, Chloe ate churros right before her Olympic run.

❇ Her dad helped her train. His engineering background helped her with the physics of each trick.

❇ Chloe's first Olympic Games in South Korea were extra special because her parents immigrated to the US from South Korea.

❇ Chloe can sing! She competed on the TV show *The Masked Singer* wearing a jellyfish costume.

# CLARA HALE
## HUMANITARIAN
April 1, 1905–
December 18, 1992
United States

The founder of Hale House, Clara Hale fostered orphaned and sick children in New York City.

## SUPERPOWER *EMPATHY*

✳ Clara helped more than 1,000 children during her life.

✳ For all of the work she did with kids, she was given the nickname Mother Hale.

✳ In 1985, President Ronald Reagan called Clara an "American hero" in a speech.

✳ Clara's three children helped out with Hale House when they got older.

✳ There is a bus depot in Harlem, New York, named after Clara.

# CLARA HOLMES
## MODEL
### Born July 30, 1980
### United Kingdom

**Clara Holmes is a fashion model, writer, and disability advocate who promotes body positivity and self-love.**

 Clara travels for adventure and tries to make sure she never visits the same place more than once.

 She is vegan. Everything from the food she eats to the clothes she wears is animal-friendly.

* Clara's professional career as a model began when she was approached on the street by scouts who chased her down because her outfit was so fabulous!

* She shares her style on Instagram and posts fashion tips on her blog, *Rollin Funky*.

# CLARA ROCKMORE

## MUSICIAN

March 9, 1911–May 10, 1998
Lithuania and United States

Clara Rockmore helped introduce an electronic instrument called a theremin to a wider audience.

+ Clara was a violin prodigy. But when she developed tendonitis as a teenager, she had to stop playing.

+ A musician plays a theremin by waving their hands between two antennae. It's very difficult to learn. Clara mastered it by keeping every other part of her body completely still while playing the instrument.

+ The first time Clara played the theremin, she was so happy to play music again she cried.

+ The inventor of the instrument, Leon Theremin, asked Clara many times to marry him. She always said no.

# CLARA SCHUMANN
## PiANIST & COMPOSER
September 13, 1819–May 20, 1896
Germany

Clara Schumann was a pianist whose career lasted for more than 60 years.

**⚡SUPERPOWER** *COMPOSITION*

- Clara was performing concerts by the time she was eight years old.

- She played music from memory, which was a rarity during her time.

- Clara gave concerts at a time when few women played music in public.

- Although she composed her own music, Clara mostly focused on showcasing her husband's music after his death.

- She was good friends with another famous composer, Johannes Brahms.

# CLAUDIA RANKINE
## POET & PLAYWRIGHT
### Born circa 1963
### Jamaica and United States

**A poet, playwright, and essayist, Claudia Rankine writes about life as a Black American and addresses race relations in the United States.**

**SUPERPOWERS** *HONESTY, INVENTIVE POETRY*

 Claudia's *Citizen* is the first and only poetry book to be a *New York Times* best seller in the nonfiction category.

 She is a great admirer of tennis player Naomi Osaka.

 Claudia loves the paintings of American artist Titus Kaphar.

 She taught literature and creative writing at several colleges before teaching poetry at Yale University.

**YOUR TURN!**

In Claudia's book *Citizen*, she uses poems, prose, and photographs to create a story. Create your own poem using more than one element. Mix your poem with photos, drawings, dialogue, or anything that shows how you see the world! Share it with friends or family.

# CLEMANTINE WAMARIYA

## AUTHOR & HUMAN RIGHTS ACTIVIST

Born 1988
Rwanda and United States

Clemantine Wamariya grew up in Rwanda during a time when a minority group was being attacked. The genocide influenced her writing and led to her advocating for refugees around the world.

★ After being separated from her family for 12 years, Clemantine was reunited with them on Oprah Winfrey's talk show.

★ A book she read that transformed her life was *Night*, by Eli Wiesel. It is his memoir of being in a concentration camp during the Holocaust.

★ President Obama made Clemantine the youngest board member of the US Holocaust Memorial Museur

★ In her spare time, Clemantin loves to do yoga.

# CLEOPATRA
## PHARAOH

69 BCE–August 12, 30 BCE
Egypt

Cleopatra was the last pharaoh to rule ancient Egypt. She ruled for more than two decades.

**⚡SUPERPOWERS** *GLAMOUR, CLEVERNESS*

★ Cleopatra spoke about 12 languages.

★ She dressed up like the Egyptian goddess Isis so everyone would know she was the ruler.

★ Although Cleopatra was born in Egypt, her family was native to what is now modern-day Greece.

★ When opposing forces tried to prevent her from meeting Julius Caesar, she hid inside a rolled-up carpet and had her servants carry it to him. She wanted to get him on her side during the civil war in Egypt.

★ Cleopatra loved to read. Homer was one of her favorite authors, and she could recite his work from memory.

# CONDOLEEZZA RICE

## — POLITICIAN —

Born November 14, 1954
United States

**Condoleezza Rice is an American diplomat and political scientist. She was the first Black woman to serve as secretary of state.**

 Condoleezza plays piano in a chamber music group and has performed with classical cellists like Yo-Yo Ma.

 She was one of the first two women to be admitted as members to the Augusta National Golf Club.

 Condoleezza has written several books, including a memoir about her childhood in Alabama.

 As the daughter of a football coach, Condolezza is a big football fan, her favorite team is the Cleveland Browns.

# CORA CORALINA

## POET & BAKER

August 20, 1889–April 10, 1985
Brazil

One of Brazil's most famous poets, Cora Coralina published her first book of poems when she was 76 years old.

* Cora became a professional poet at the age of 60.

* To earn money, she sold homemade baked goods outside her home, along with her poems.

* She is most known for baking cakes, but she also sold sausages.

* Cora Coralina is not her real name—she came up with it when she was a child.

* Although she moved to São Paulo when she got married, Cora eventually returned to her childhood home in Goiás to live out the rest of her life.

# CORRIE TEN BOOM
## watchmaker

April 15, 1892–April 15, 1983
The Netherlands
and United States

**SUPERPOWERS**
*Bravery,*
**ATTENTION TO DETAIL**

**Corrie ten Boom was a watchmaker who helped Jewish people escape the Nazis during World War II.**

* Corrie was from a family of watchmakers. Her father and grandfather were watchmakers before her.

* She was the first licensed female watchmaker in Holland.

* She constructed a hidden room in her bedroom where Jewish people could hide.

* Corrie wrote a book about her experiences during World War II. Later, it was made into a movie.

* Her full name was Cornelia, after her mother. However, she went by Corrie her whole life.

# DANNI WASHINGTON

## OCEAN ADVOCATE

Born December 30, 1986
United States

Danni Washington is a climate activist and TV personality who fights to keep oceans free from pollution.

Some of Danni's favorite ocean activities are scuba diving and stand-up paddleboarding.

Danni is the first Black woman to host her own science TV show.

She first got the idea of pursuing a career in marine biology when she watched the movie *Free Willy* as a kid.

Danni often wears a mermaid tail when she swims. She calls herself and her clothing brand the Mocha Mermaid.

Outside of the water, she loves to cook and quilt.

# DIANE VON FÜRSTENBERG

## Fashion Designer

Born December 31, 1946
Belgium and United States

**Diane von Fürstenberg is a fashion designer
most known for her iconic wrap dress.**

 To come up with the wrap dress, Diane combined a skirt with a wrap shirt.

 Clothing from her fashion company is available in more than 70 countries.

 Although she loves music, Diane prefers the peacefulness of total silence.

* Her favorite book is *The Little Prince* by Antoine de Saint-Exupéry.

* She became a princess when she married her first husband, a prince.

Diane's designs are known for their iconic chain link-patterned fabric. Try designing your own fabric with tie-dye! Find rubber bands, some fabric, and cloth dye in several colors. Wrap the rubber bands around different sections of the fabric.

Follow the directions on the package of dye. Then, when you are ready and with an adult's help, submerge different sections of the fabric in whichever colors you like.

Take the fabric out of the dye and let it sit for about eight hours. Remove the rubber bands and wash and dry your fabric. See what cool patterns you've made!

# DOMINIQUE JACKSON

## actor

Born March 20, 1975
Trinidad and Tobago
and United States

Dominique Jackson is a transgender actor known for her role on the TV show *Pose*.

* Growing up, Dominique related to characters like the X-Men and She-Ra, Princess of Power, and their stories of perseverance.

* Seeing Black supermodels like Iman and Tyra Banks inspired Dominique to enter the modeling industry.

* She mentors queer young adults of color and makes sure they feel supported.

* Dominique believes in the power of shoes! She has a T-shirt line called Get the Shoes Baby.

### SUPERPOWERS
*SOUL, SOPHISTICATION*

# DOREEN SIMMONS

## SPOrTS COMMENTATOR

May 29, 1932–April 23, 2018
United Kingdom and Japan

**Doreen Simmons was a sumo wrestling commentator for English television.**

## ⚡SUPERPOWERS

### OBSERVATION, LANGUAGE SKILLS

* Doreen commented on sumo wrestling matches for 25 years.

* For her contributions to Japanese culture, the government awarded Doreen the Order of the Rising Sun—one of the country's highest honors.

* To celebrate her 68th birthday, she went bungee jumping.

* Doreen said the best way to learn about sumo is to watch teen wrestlers who are also just starting out.

# EDMONIA LEWIS

## SCULPTOR

Circa 1844–
September 17, 1907
United States and Italy

Edmonia Lewis was the first Black and Indigenous woman to achieve international recognition as a sculptor.

## ⚡SUPERPOWERS CREATIVITY, REALISTIC SCULPTING

✦ Edmonia was part Ojibwe and went by her Indigenous name, Wildfire, when she was a kid.

✦ Many of her sculptures related to her Black and Indigenous heritage.

✦ One of her most famous works is a sculpture of Cleopatra, which was lost for nearly 100 years.

✦ Edmonia's sculptures can be found in many museums today, including the Metropolitan Museum of Art.

# EILEEN GRAY

## architect &
## furniture designer

August 9, 1878–October 31, 1976
Ireland and France

With her keen eye for architecture, Eileen Gray helped pioneer the modern design movement.

### ⚡ SUPERPOWERS *elegance, craftsmanship*

✦ Eileen was often inspired by Japanese design and infused many of its elements into her work.

✦ Her favorite material to work with was lacquer.

✦ Eileen received long-overdue recognition for her designs when she was 94 years old.

✦ The "Dragons" armchair she designed is the most expensive chair ever to be auctioned off. It sold for $28.3 million!

# ELEANOR ROOSEVELT

## POLITICIAN

October 11, 1884–
November 7, 1962
United States

During her time as First Lady of the United States, Eleanor Roosevelt was a champion for human rights. She eventually became a delegate to the United Nations.

* Eleanor is the longest-serving First Lady. She held the position from 1933 to 1945.

* While she was in prep school, she played field hockey.

* From 1935 until her death in 1962, Eleanor wrote a column called "My Day" six days a week.

* She starred in commercials, including ones for mattresses, hot dogs, and butter!

### SUPERPOWERS

advocacy, compassic

# ELISABETH KÜBLER-ROSS

## PSYCHIATRIST

July 8, 1926–August 24, 2004
Switzerland and United States

Psychologist Elisabeth Kübler-Ross developed a theory about how people deal with death. It is known as the five stages of grief.

## SUPERPOWERS
### INTELLIGENCE, COMMUNICATION

* Elisabeth was one of a set of triplets.

* When she was 13 years old, Elisabeth volunteered to help war victims during World War II.

* Her father didn't want her to become a doctor. Elisabeth left home at age 16 to follow her dreams of going to medical school.

* *Time* magazine named her one of the most important thinkers of the 20th century.

# ELIZABETH I
## QUEEN
September 7, 1533–March 24, 1603
United Kingdom

Elizabeth I was the Queen of England from 1558 to 1603. She is often regarded as one of the greatest rulers in England's history.

## ⚡SUPERPOWERS *WIT, STRATEGIC THINKING*

+ When Elizabeth's sister Mary was queen, she imprisoned Elizabeth. Mary thought Elizabeth would try to steal her crown.

+ Elizabeth loved sweets, especially candied violets.

+ She knew seven different languages.

+ She loved the plays of William Shakespeare and often hosted performances of them.

# EMILIE SNETHLAGE

## ORNITHOLOGIST

April 13, 1868–November 25, 1929
Germany and Brazil

Emilie Snethlage spent her career in the Amazon rain forest studying birds and other animals.

**SUPERPOWER** *OBSERVATION*

- When she was in college, Emilie had to take classes behind a screen because women were not allowed to officially enroll.

- During her career, she identified more than 60 species of birds.

- Emilie had to amputate her own finger after a piranha bit her and the wound became infected.

- She discovered a new species of bird, eventually named after her, called Snethlage's tody-tyrant.

# EMMY NOETHER

## MATHEMATICIAN

March 23, 1882–
April 14, 1935
Germany
and United States

Emmy Noether developed a physics theorem that made her one of the most important mathematicians of the 20th century.

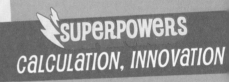

## SUPERPOWERS
## CALCULATION, INNOVATION

★ Emmy established Noether's theorem, which addresses symmetry in the universe.

★ When she started teaching at a university, she was not getting paid, because she was a woman.

★ She helped develop abstract algebra.

★ Albert Einstein was a great admirer of Emmy and her work. He called her a genius.

★ Emmy didn't like to follow formal lesson plans with her students. She preferred to have conversations that would lead to great ideas.

# EUFROSINA CRUZ

## ACTIVIST & POLITICIAN

Born January 1, 1979
Mexico

Eufrosina Cruz is the first Indigenous woman to be elected to the state congress of Oaxaca. She fights for equality for women and Indigenous peoples.

**SUPERPOWER** *resilience*

⭐ When she was young, Eufrosina sold candy and gum in order to pay for her schooling.

⭐ She pushed the change in the Mexican constitution that made it possible for Indigenous people to vote without limitations.

⭐ Although Eufrosina won an election to be mayor of her town, the town board tore up her ballots because she is a woman.

⭐ She carries a white lily with her to remind herself that, like the flower, Indigenous women are natural, beautiful, and resilient.

# FLEUR JONG

## PARALYMPIC LONG JUMPER & SPRINTER

Born December 17, 1995
The Netherlands

Fleur Jong won a gold medal at the 2020 Paralympics in the long jump and set world records in both the 100-meter dash and the long jump.

### ⚡ SUPERPOWERS
### AGILITY, DETERMINATION

Fleur was one of the flag bearers for the Netherlands at the 2020 Paralympics.

Her legs were amputated when she was 16 because she had a bacterial infection.

Fleur trained for the long jump for only a month before she started competing.

She loves to read and solve puzzles.

# FLORENCE CHADWICK

## SWIMMER

November 9, 1918–
March 15, 1995
United States

A long-distance and open-water swimmer, Florence Chadwick was the first woman to swim the English Channel both ways.

## ⚡SUPERPOWER STAMINA

* Florence began competitive swimming at six years old.

* During her career, she broke record times of both men and women swimmers before her.

* A strait is a narrow waterway that connects two big bodies of water—and Florence swam many of them. She was the first woman to swim the length of the Strait of Gibraltar, the Bosporus, and the Dardenelles.

* She put on swimming shows for the military during World War II.

* She was often a consultant for swimming scenes in movies.

# FLORENCE GRIFFITH JOYNER

## Sprinter

December 21, 1959–
September 21, 1998
United States

Florence Griffith Joyner
holds the world records
for both the 100-meter and
200-meter dashes.

* Before Florence devoted herself to running, she was a bank teller.

* Her nickname was Flo-Jo.

* She designed the uniforms for the basketball team the Indiana Pacers.

* Many knew Florence for her fun style on the track. She often wore one-legged unitards, long nails, and jewelry as she ran.

* She was the first woman in the US to win four medals in track and field at a single Olympic Games.

# FLORENCE NIGHTINGALE
## NURSE
### May 12, 1820–August 13, 1910
### United Kingdom

Using techniques that became the start of modern nursing, Florence Nightingale helped wounded soldiers during the Crimean War.

## ⚡SUPERPOWERS *NURTURING, GRIT*

* Florence was known as the Lady with the Lamp because she carried a lamp with her while checking on patients at night.

* She reduced the death rate of a cholera outbreak by implementing hygiene practices that didn't exist at the time, like regular handwashing.

* Florence was named for the city where she was born: Florence, Italy.

* She had an owl called Athena, named after the city where she found her pet: Athens, Greece.

# FRIDA KAHLO

## painter

July 6, 1907–July 13, 1954
Mexico

**Frida Kahlo is known for her striking self-portraits and the bold colors she used on her canvases.**

* Frida taught herself to paint while lying down after she was injured in a bus accident.

* Her home, called La Casa Azul, was painted a vibrant blue.

* One version of Mexico's 500-peso bill shows a portrait of Frida. Her longtime partner, Diego Rivera, was featured on the other side of the bill.

* Frida liked a hairless breed of dog called the Xoloitzcuintli. (That's pronounced *SHO-lo-eetz-QUEENT-lee!*)

Frida was famous for the self-portraits she painted. Try making a self-portrait of your own. You could sketch with pencils, collage with magazine clippings, paint with watercolors, or even sculpt yourself out of clay. Find a mirror, gather your art supplies, and get started. Like Frida, don't be afraid to be bold and colorful!

# FRIEDA BELINFANTE
## CELLIST & CONDUCTOR
### May 10, 1904–April 26, 1995
### The Netherlands and United States

Frieda Belinfante was a talented cellist and the first woman conductor in Europe.

+ Frieda disguised herself as a man to escape the Nazis during World War II.

+ At a refugee camp in Switzerland, she found a cello and performed a concert.

+ As the director of the Philharmonic Society of Orange County, in California, Frieda made concerts free so as many people as possible could hear the music.

+ In 1987, the Orange County Board of Supervisors declared February 19 as Frieda Belinfante Day to honor her contributions to the local music community.

# GABBY DOUGLAS

## GYMNAST

Born December 31, 1995
United States

Gabby Douglas was the first Black gymnast to win a gold medal in the individual all-around event at the Olympics.

**⚡SUPERPOWERS** *OPTIMISM, STRENGTH*

- Gabby's nickname is the "Flying Squirrel" because of how high she flies on the uneven bars.

- Gabby first became interested in gymnastics while practicing cartwheels with her sister.

- Between her start in gymnastics at six years old and her first Olympics, Gabby trained for more than 18,000 hours!

- The company that created Barbie designed a doll to look like Gabby.

# GAE AULENTI
## architect & designer
### December 4, 1927–
### October 31, 2012
### Italy

Gae Aulenti's experimental designs for buildings and furniture made her one of the greatest architects in history.

* When she was studying architecture, Gae was one of only two women in her class of 20.

* She used geometric shapes and clean lines in her work.

* People loved her lamps, especially her iconic Pipistrello lampshade, which is shaped like batwings.

* Gae was on the editorial team of a design magazine before eventually becoming its art director.

* *Piazza Gae Aulenti* is a square in Milan, Italy, dedicated to her.

## SUPERPOWERS
### SPIRIT, GEOMETRY

# GEORGIA O'KEEFFE

## painter

November 15, 1887–
March 6, 1986
United States

Modernist artist Georgia O'Keeffe is known for her close-up paintings of flowers and New Mexico landscapes.

## ⚡ SUPERPOWERS BOLDNESS, COMPOSITION

+ For Georgia's contributions to the art world, she is known as the Mother of American Modernism.

+ One of her paintings sold for $44.4 million. It was the most expensive painting ever sold by a female artist.

+ Although Georgia is well known for her paintings of flowers, they only make up about 200 of her 2,000-piece collection.

+ Her favorite place to paint was in her car!

# GIUSI NICOLINI

## POLITICIAN

Born March 5, 1961
Italy

During her time as mayor of Lampedusa, Giusi Nicolini made efforts to protect the island's natural landscape and welcomed refugees without bias.

## ⚡SUPERPOWER *EMPATHY*

★ When she was young, Giusi enjoyed exploring cliffs and caves with her siblings.

★ Although she is best known for being the mayor of Lampedusa, Giusi was also mayor of the island of Linosa.

★ She is sometimes called "the Lioness" for her tireless efforts for refugees.

★ Giusi received the UNESCO Peace Prize for her work on Lampedusa.

# GLADYS KALEMA-ZIKUSOKA

## — WILDLIFE VETERINARIAN — & CONSERVATIONIST

Born January 8, 1970
Uganda

**Veterinarian Gladys Kalema-Zikusoka is one of the leading conservationists working to prevent the extinction of mountain gorillas.**

★ When she was 12, Gladys set up a wildlife club in her school.

★ At 25 years old, she became Uganda's first wildlife veterinarian.

★ In the mid-1990s, the mountain gorilla population was around 600. Gladys's efforts have increased the population by almost 400.

★ Gladys's role model is her mother Rhoda, who was one of the first women to join Uganda's parliament.

⚡**SUPERPOWERS**
*LOGIC, COMPASSION*

# GLORIA ESTEFAN

## SINGER

Born September 1, 1957
Cuba and United States

Gloria Estefan is a Cuban American singer whose career has lasted more than 40 years.

## ⚡SUPERPOWERS
### AMBITION, HARMONIES

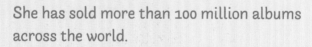

+ Gloria is known as the Queen of Latin Pop.

+ She has sold more than 100 million albums across the world.

+ The Broadway musical *On Your Feet!* was inspired by the lives of Gloria and her husband Emilio.

+ In 2017, Gloria received a Kennedy Center Honor. She was the first Cuban American to receive the award.

# GLORIA STEINEM

## JOURNALIST & POLITICAL ACTIVIST

Born March 25, 1934
United States

Gloria Steinem was a leading figure in the US feminist movement in the 1960s and 1970s.

## ⚡SUPERPOWERS
### ADVOCACY, BOLDNESS

+ As a child, Gloria traveled all over the United States with her family while her dad worked as a traveling antique salesman.

+ Reading the book *Little Women* helped shape her views on women and their independence.

+ In 1971, Gloria started the first feminist magazine in the United States. She called it *Ms.*

+ Soccer star Megan Rapinoe once gifted Gloria a soccer ball signed by the members of the US Women's National Team.

# GOLDA MEIR

## — POLITICIAN —

May 3, 1898–December 8, 1978
Ukraine, United States, and Israel

As of 2022, Golda Meir was the first and only woman to be the prime minister of Israel.

## ⚡SUPERPOWER *eloquence*

✦ Golda had to convince her parents to let her go to high school. They wanted her to get married instead.

✦ She taught children reading, writing, and history at a Yiddish school.

✦ Golda changed her last name from Meyerson to Meir, which means "illuminate" in Hebrew.

✦ Before she became prime minister, Golda was ready to retire. She wanted to focus on her grandchildren and have a quieter life.

✦ She was the first person to receive an Israeli passport.

# GRACE HOPPER
## COMPUTER SCIENTIST
December 9, 1906–January 1, 1992
United States

Grace Hopper's computer programming helped the United States decode secret messages from other countries during World War II.

## ⚡SUPERPOWERS *CALCULATION, FOCUS*

+ As a child, Grace was always trying to figure out how things worked. Once, she even took apart seven clocks before her mother stopped her.

+ She regularly woke up at 5:00 a.m. to work on computer coding.

+ When a moth flew into a computer, Grace helped popularize the terms "bug" and "debugging" to describe computer malfunctions.

+ She was known as Amazing Grace for her computer talents and important contributions to the country.

# GRACE O'MALLEY
## PIRATE
Circa 1530–1603
Ireland

Grace O'Malley was an Irish pirate queen who commanded a fleet of ships and evaded British rule during the 16th century.

* Grace's father wouldn't let her go with him on an expedition because she was a girl, so she disguised herself as a boy and snuck onto the ship! Onboard, she proved she could work just as hard as the men.

* According to legend, she led the capture of a ship an hour after giving birth.

* When Grace met Queen Elizabeth I, it is rumored that she refused to bow down to her.

* Grace's Irish name is Gráinne Ní Mháille.

## ⚡SUPERPOWERS
### BRAVERY, LEADERSHIP

# GRETA THUNBERG

## CLIMATE ACTIVIST

Born January 3, 2003
Sweden

reta Thunberg's school strike challenged world leaders to ake action on climate reform.

* When Greta was 15 years old, she stood outside the Swedish parliament every day, refusing to go back to school until the government followed through on their plan to reduce carbon emissions.

* To be environmentally friendly, Greta does not travel by airplanes, gas-fueled cars, or motorized boats.

* She has Asperger's syndrome, which she describes as a gift and superpower.

* Greta is the youngest person to be named *Time*'s person of the year.

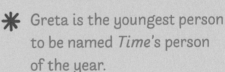

**SUPERPOWERS**
courage, persuasion

# HARRIET TUBMAN

## FREEDOM FIGHTER

Circa 1822–
March 10, 1913
United States

Harriet Tubman helped more than 70 enslaved people escape to freedom using the Underground Railroad.

## ⚡ SUPERPOWER *HEROISM*

⭐ While escaping from enslavement, Harriet looked at the stars to figure out which direction was north.

⭐ Harriet was born Araminta but changed her name to Harriet in honor of her mother.

⭐ In 1896, she opened a nursing home in New York.

⭐ During the Civil War, she treated soldiers wounded on the battlefield.

⭐ She worked with Susan B. Anthony during the women's suffrage movement.

# HATSHEPSUT

## PHARAOH

Circa 1508-1458 BCE
Egypt

**Hatshepsut was the first woman pharaoh in Egypt to achieve the full power of the position.**

**SUPERPOWER** *MYSTERY*

- Hatshepsut proclaimed herself king. Sometimes she wore men's clothing or even a fake beard to emphasize her power.

- She ruled Egypt for 20 years—a long reign by ancient standards. Her reign was peaceful.

- Hatshepsut renamed herself Maatkare, which translates to "Truth (maat) is the Soul (ka) of the Sun God (Re)" to symbolize how she was meant to rule.

- Vandals smashed her statues, and the pharoah who took her place removed her name from official records in efforts to erase her from history.

# HAZEL SCOTT

## MUSICIAN & ACTIVIST

June 11, 1920–October 2, 1981
Trinidad and Tobago
and United States

**Hazel Scott was a musician and activist who fought the discrimination against and segregation of Black people.**

 **SUPERPOWERS** *CONVICTION, PIANO SKILLS*

- At eight years old, Hazel became the youngest music student admitted to the Juilliard School.

- She was the first Black woman to host her own television show.

- Hazel refused to perform in segregated theaters.

- When she was in movies, she also refused to play a maid or appear dirty on film. She did not want to show audiences bad or stereotyped versions of Black people.

**YOUR TURN!**

Hazel spoke seven languages! What languages would you like to learn? Pick five words. With an adult, look up the translation of each word in three different languages. See if the words have anything in common with each other. Memorize them and share them with your friends.

# HEDY LAMARR

## actor & INVENTOR

November 9, 1914–
January 19, 2000
Austria
and United States

In addition to being a renowned Hollywood actor, Hedy Lamarr invented a device that later became the basis for wireless technology.

* Hedy's interest in inventions began at age five, when she took apart a music box and put it back together.

* Hedy could speak four languages by the time she was 10.

* She co-invented a secret communications system that changed the radio frequencies of secret messages so enemies couldn't decode them. Today, it is used in satellites, cell phones, and other technology.

* Hedy never made any money on her inventions.

* The character designs for Snow White and Catwoman were inspired by Hedy.

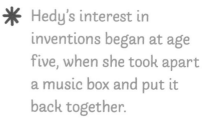

## SUPERPOWERS
### BEAUTY, BRAINS

# HELEN KELLER
## ACTIVIST
June 27, 1880–June 1, 1968
United States

Helen Keller was an activist and author who traveled the world giving speeches and championing the rights of people with disabilities.

**SUPERPOWERS** *PATIENCE, SELF-CONFIDENCE*

* When she was 19 months old, Helen suffered from a bad fever that left her deaf and blind.

* Her teacher, Anne Sullivan, taught her how to talk by signing letters onto the palm of her hand.

* Helen learned five languages in Braille—a writing system that uses raised dots. People with visual impairments read Braille by feeling the dots with their fingers.

* Mark Twain, the author of *The Adventures of Tom Sawyer*, was a friend of Helen's and loved her sense of humor.

* Helen loved dogs. When asked what she would like to see if she had three days of eyesight, she wrote, "I should like to look into the loyal, trusting eyes of my dogs."

# HIDILYN DIAZ
## WEIGHTLIFTER
Born February 20, 1991
The Philippines

World-class weightlifter Hidilyn Diaz won the Philippines's first ever Olympic gold medal.

**⚡SUPERPOWER** *vigor*

 When she was 11, Hidilyn tried weightlifting for the first time. She was with her older brothers, and she could lift more than them!

 Her family couldn't afford equipment, so she trained by lifting wood, metal hubcaps, and blocks of concrete.

During the Olympics in 2021, she lifted 227 kilograms (an Olympic record), which equals 500 pounds!

 She serves in the Philippine Air Force as a staff sergeant.

 Her favorite dish is *kare-kare*, a stew made with peanut sauce, pork, beef, and vegetables.

**YOUR TURN!**

Grab a grown-up and a bunch of books. Hold your arms out straight with your palms facing up. Ask your grown-up to put one book on each hand and count to 20. Take a rest and do it again. If holding up one book is easy, try it with two! Once you've mastered two books, try three.

# HYPATIA

## MATHEMATICIAN & PHILOSOPHER

Circa 370–March 415
Egypt

Brilliant astronomer and mathematician Hypatia was one of the first women to study and teach math, science, and philosophy.

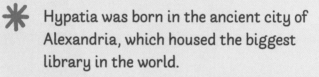

**SUPERPOWER** *INTELLIGENCE*

* Hypatia was born in the ancient city of Alexandria, which housed the biggest library in the world.

* She refused to wear traditional women's clothes and dressed in scholars' robes whenever she taught.

* Hypatia made and used a device known as an astrolabe. It calculated the position of the sun, moon, and stars at any given time.

* She never married. She wanted to devote her life to academics.

# IBTIHAJ MUHAMMAD

## Fencer

Born December 4, 1985
United States

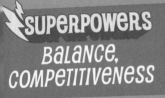

**SUPERPOWERS**
**BALANCE,**
**COMPETITIVENESS**

**Ibtihaj Muhammad is the first woman to wear a hijab while representing the United States at the Olympics.**

 At age 13, Ibtihaj started fencing—a sport that includes fighting with swords called foils, épées, or sabres.

 In 2016, she won a bronze medal with her sabre team at the Summer Olympics in Rio de Janeiro.

* She is a best-selling author and speaks publicly about how to overcome barriers for women and girls in sports.

* A Barbie doll was modeled after Ibtihaj. The doll wears a fencing mask and uniform.

# IDA B. WELLS

## JOURNALIST
July 16, 1862–
March 25, 1931
United States

Ida B. Wells was a pioneer of investigative journalism, a crusader against lynching, and a fierce fighter for voting rights.

**SUPERPOWERS** DETERMINATION, GUTS

★ Ida's parents passed away when she was 16. She became a teacher to support her five younger siblings. She lied and said she was 18 to get the job.

★ A conductor once removed Ida from a train car that was for white people only. "He tried to drag me out of the seat," she wrote, "but . . . I fastened my teeth in the back of his hand." Later, she sued the railway company and won!

★ Ida helped found several civil rights organizations, including the National Association for the Advancement of Colored People (NAACP).

★ She fought for women's right to vote and fair hiring practices for jobs, and even ran for Illinois state senate.

★ There is a statue of her in Chicago—the first in the city dedicated to a Black woman.

# IMAN
## SUPERMODEL & BUSINESSWOMAN
### Born July 25, 1955
### Somalia and United States

One of the world's first Black supermodels, Iman uses her influence to tell people about the beauty and challenges of Somalia.

⭐ As a little girl, Iman and her family were forced to flee Somalia because of a war that is still going on.

⭐ Iman's career began after a famous photographer noticed her in Kenya and asked to photograph her. She used the money she earned from the photo shoot to pay for school.

⭐ Iman started her own line of cosmetics for women of color.

⭐ She's built schools and provided support for refugee families in Africa.

⭐ Iman likes to wake up early. Her favorite time of day is 5:30 a.m.

# INSOONI

## SINGER

Born April 5, 1957
South Korea

Born Kim In-soon, Insooni is a South Korean singer who has helped biracial kids get an education free from bullying.

⭐ Born to a South Korean mother and Black American father, Insooni was bullied as a child for being biracial and having darker skin than her classmates.

⭐ She sang her best-selling song "Let Everyone Shine" at the opening ceremonies of the 2018 Winter Olympics, which were hosted by her country.

⭐ Insooni founded the Hae Mil School to provide a better learning experience for children of mixed ethnic backgrounds. Tuition is paid for from her concert money!

⭐ She has starred in musicals, including *Cats* and *Chicago*.

# IRENA SENDLEROWA
## War Hero
### February 15, 1910–May 12, 2008
### Poland

**Irena Sendlerowa's heroic actions during World War II saved thousands of lives.**

**SUPERPOWER** *KINDNESS*

★ During World War II, Irena gave Jewish children fake Christian names and found families who would keep them safe.

★ In just three months, she saved more than 2,500 children.

★ Irena wrote the children's real and fake names on slips of paper, put the slips in jars, and buried them. After the war, she dug up the jars and reunited many of the children with their families.

★ There is a play about her called *Life in a Jar*.

★ Upon receiving an award for her efforts, she had to perform the tradition of drinking a glass of lemon juice while smiling!

# ISABEL ALLENDE
## author
Born August 2, 1942
Peru, Chile, and United States

**Isabel Allende is known for writing in a style called magical realism, which mixes elements of fantasy into realistic stories.**

## SUPERPOWER *IMAGINATION*

* Isabel was a journalist until her grandfather got sick. A letter she wrote to him ended up becoming her first novel, *The House of the Spirits*. One of the characters can move furniture with her mind.

* January 8 is the day she started writing the letter, and it is now the day she begins each new project.

* Isabel had to flee with her husband and children when rebels overthrew Chile's elected president, Salvador Allende. Salvador was her uncle!

* The Isabel Allende Foundation, which is funded by profits from her books, empowers women worldwide by protecting them from poverty, disease, and violence.

YOUR TURN!

In magical realism, fantasy and real life exist together, and the magic that exists does not surprise the characters. It is just a regular part of their world. Try writing about your day at school, but add some magical elements to your story.

# ISADORA DUNCAN

## Dancer

May 27, 1877–September 14, 1927
United States

A pioneering performer, Isadora Duncan is known as the Mother of Modern Dance.

✦ Isadora's family was poor, so Isadora started teaching dance lessons to local children to earn money. She was just six years old at the time!

✦ She didn't like ballet. She thought it had too many rules and was "ugly and against nature."

✦ Isadora created a modern style that was free and natural. She wore loose white dresses with long scarves to show off her flowing movements.

✦ Isadora didn't believe in marriage, and she often spoke about equal rights for women.

# ISATOU CEESAY

## ACTIVIST & SOCIAL ENTREPRENEUR

Born December 30, 1972
The Gambia

**SUPERPOWER**
craftiness

Isatou Ceesay helped women, her village, her community, and her country by transforming trash into treasure.

✦ When she was young, Isatou would make dolls out of leftover scraps of cloth and wood.

✦ She opened up her village's first recycling center, where she collected plastic bags to make into "plarn," or plastic yarn, which was then used to make purses.

✦ Her movement grew to include more than 2,000 women from 40 communities.

✦ In 2015, The Gambia's government finally banned plastic bags.

# ISSA RAE
## actor, writer, & producer
Born January 12, 1985
United States

Award-winning actor and writer Issa Rae created the hit TV series *Insecure*.

* Once, all of Issa's filmmaking equipment, films, and scripts were stolen from her apartment.

* Issa wrote, directed, and starred in a web series called *Awkward Black Girl*. She wanted to tell stories that didn't include any of the Black stereotypes she grew up watching as a child.

* *Awkward Black Girl* was the inspiration for her show *Insecure*, which ran for five years and won an Emmy Award.

* She started a company to support Black writers and help bring their projects to life.

* Her favorite meal of the day is breakfast.

# JAMIE MARGOLIN

## CLIMATE ACTIVIST

Born December 10, 2001
United States

Jamie Margolin started the worldwide youth movement Zero Hour.

* Jamie founded Zero Hour at 15 years old to encourage other young people to fight for climate justice.

* Jamie's organization is called Zero Hour because, as she writes, "[Now] is the only chance we will ever have to save ourselves . . . "

* Jamie sued Washington State for denying her generation's constitutional rights to live in a safe environment.

* She wants to make films and TV shows. Her web series, *Art Majors*, is about a group of queer friends navigating heartbreak.

# JANE AUSTEN
## author
December 16, 1775–
July 18, 1817
United Kingdom

Jane Austen is regarded as one of the most famous and beloved writers of English literature. During her lifetime, her fans didn't know who she was. She published her books anonymously.

## ⚡SUPERPOWERS
## irony, self-expression

When she was a kid, Jane put on plays at home with her six brothers and older sister.

At the time, it wasn't acceptable for a woman of her status to make money from writing. Jane's first novel, *Sense and Sensibility*, states that it was written "By a Lady."

Jane was the first female writer to appear on British currency.

Fans of her books often call themselves Janeites or Austenites.

# JANE GOODALL
## PRIMATOLOGIST
Born April 3, 1934
United Kingdom

Jane Goodall is an expert on chimpanzees.
She has spent her career teaching the world
about primates and how to protect their
environment so they can thrive.

+ As a child, Jane loved to read
adventure stories about the
character Tarzan, who lived
in the jungle. Her favorite toy
was a stuffed chimpanzee
named Jubilee.

+ At the age of 26, she got her
first opportunity to study
chimpanzees in their natural
environment in Tanzania.

+ She'd share bananas with the
chimps she studied. It was her
"Banana Club."

+ She learned that chimps
use tools, have rituals, show
affection, get in fights, and
even adopt orphaned baby
chimps.

# JAWAHIR JEWELS ROBLE

## REFEREE

Born circa 1994
Somalia and United Kingdom

Jawahir Jewels Roble is the first female Muslim soccer referee in the United Kingdom.

## ⚡ SUPERPOWER DEDICATION

- ✦ Jawahir—known as JJ—grew up playing soccer, first in her war-torn home country of Somalia and later as a refugee in England.

- ✦ A national newspaper called her "the most remarkable referee in England."

- ✦ JJ wears a head covering called a hijab. She has had to overcome prejudice on the field.

- ✦ Her dream is to one day train Somalia's soccer team.

# JAZZ JENNINGS

## LGBTQIA+ ACTIVIST

Born October 6, 2000
United States

Jazz Jennings paved the way for many young transgender people and shared her experiences on the reality series *I Am Jazz*.

- Jazz always knew she was a girl and was able to verbalize it by age two.

- In 2017, she became the inspiration for the first transgender doll, which was modeled after her.

- Jazz and her parents founded the TransKids Purple Rainbow Foundation to help transgender and nonbinary kids thrive.

- Jazz loves mermaids.

**SUPERPOWERS**
*COMPASSION, OUTSPOKENNESS*

# JESSAMYN STANLEY
## YOGA TEACHER
### Born June 27, 1987
### United States

**Jessamyn Stanley is a body positivity advocate who believes in the power of yoga and self-acceptance.**

## ⚡SUPERPOWERS *CONFIDENCE, FLEXIBILITY*

 When Jessamyn wanted to play team sports, she was told she was slow and uncoordinated. So she signed up for a yoga class instead.

 She's shared her experiences and described the power of yoga in two books: *Every Body Yoga* and *Yoke*.

 Jessamyn started an online community to help people feel better about their bodies through the practice of yoga.

 She has cats and a chihuahua named Babyshark.

 She collects vintage furniture.

The first time Jessamyn tried yoga, she hated it. She later grew to love it. Her younger self would have been amazed that she grew up to be a yoga instructor. Think of one thing you're scared to try. Pretend you are all grown up and write a letter from your future self explaining how you got over the fear.

your TUrN!

# JESSICA WATSON

## sailor

Born May 18, 1993
Australia

After spending 210 days at sea, Jessica Watson became the youngest person to sail around the world alone without stopping.

+ Jessica used to be afraid of the water.

+ At 16, she painted *Ella's Pink Lady* (her boat) bright pink, packed it with food and water, and set sail around the world.

+ During her voyage, she faced 30-foot waves and cyclone-strength winds. Her boat got knocked over several times.

+ Jessica finished her round-the-world journey three days before her 17th birthday. More than 75,000 people waited for her at the harbor.

+ In 2010, a documentary called *210 Days: Around the World with Jessica Watson* was released.

# JOAN BEAUCHAMP PROCTER

## ZOOLOGIST

August 5, 1897–September 20, 1931
United Kingdom

**In a time when women weren't encouraged to be scientists, Joan Beauchamp Procter was a famous herpetologist—an expert on reptiles and amphibians.**

**SUPERPOWER** *CURIOSITY*

- As a child, Joan traveled everywhere with her Dalmatian wall lizard. She also kept a baby crocodile in the family's bathtub and took it to school once!

- Joan had a reptile house built. People came from all over to watch her handle python snakes.

- She brought her favorite Komodo dragon to children's tea parties.

- Two species of reptiles have been named after Joan: *Buhoma procterae*, a type of snake, and *Testudo procterae*, a type of tortoise.

# JOAN JETT
## — rock star —
Born September 22, 1958
United States

**Joan Jett has been a pioneer for women who rock! Her never-give-up attitude helped her break through the male-dominated world of rock music.**

## SUPERPOWERS
### DEFIANCE, GUITAR SHREDS

* Joan was just 15 years old when she started the all-girl, punk rock band The Runaways.

* When Joan pitched an album to music companies, she was turned down 23 times! She started her own label, becoming the first female artist to own an independent record company.

* Her song "I Love Rock 'n' Roll" hit #1 on the Billboard charts in 1982 and is still a popular song today.

* She's listed in *Rolling Stone* magazine as one of the 100 Greatest Guitarists of all time.

# JOSEPHINE BAKER
## entertainer & activist
### June 3, 1906–April 12, 1975
### United States and France

Born into poverty in the segregated United States, Josephine Baker became one of the most famous entertainers in France. She used that fame to help win a world war and fight for civil rights.

**SUPERPOWERS** *HUMOR, ADVOCACY*

- Josephine moved to France at age 19. Two years later, she became the first Black woman to star in a feature film.

- During World War II, she carried messages for the French Resistance using invisible ink on her sheet music.

- Josephine lent her voice to the civil rights movement in the US. She pointed out that in France, she could move freely and go to any hotel or restaurant she wanted.

- Her favorite food was spaghetti. She would make it for her family every Sunday night.

- She had a pet cheetah!

# JOY BUOLAMWINI

## COMPUTER SCIENTIST

Born January 23, 1990
Canada, Ghana,
and United States

Digital activist Joy Buolamwini
uses art and research to
fight discrimination in
computer software.

**SUPERPOWERS**
*LOGIC, CREATIVITY*

- Joy found that some artificial intelligence, or AI, systems were better at recognizing male faces than female faces. They struggled even more to recognize dark-skinned women.

- She showed that well-known companies had AI systems that misidentifed the faces of famous Black women like Oprah Winfrey, Michelle Obama, and Serena Williams.

- Joy advises politicians, serves on companies' panels, and encourages women of color to get jobs in technology.

- She calls herself a "poet of code" for the way she integrates engineering with language and art.

# JUDITH JAMISON
## DANCER & CHOREOGRAPHER
### Born May 10, 1943
### United States

With dedication, elegance, and strength, Judith Jamison became one of the most prominent figures in modern dance.

- Judith was a tall, gangly child with so much energy that her mother put her in ballet lessons just to tire her out.

- She went to college to study psychology, but she couldn't stop thinking about dancing. She left school to dance professionally.

- At 22, Judith joined the Alvin Ailey American Dance Theater and became a star by combining elements of ballet with modern dance.

## SUPERPOWERS
### ELEGANCE, EMOTION

- After Alvin's death, Judith returned to the Alvin Ailey American Dance Theater and became the first Black woman to direct a modern dance company.

- One of her best-known dances, "Cry," was choreographed by Alvin and dedicated to all Black women.

# JULIA "BUTTERFLY" HILL

## activist & author

### Born February 18, 1974
### United States

**Julia "Butterfly" Hill went out on a limb (literally!) in order to save the California redwoods that she dearly loved.**

**⚡SUPERPOWER** *TENACITY*

 Julia got the nickname Butterfly when she was seven. A butterfly landed on her hand when she was hiking and stayed with her the entire day.

 At the age of 23, Julia met a group of protesters who were trying to prevent a logging company from cutting down redwoods. She volunteered to be a tree-sitter.

 To protect a tree, Julia lived 180 feet up in the air, on a tiny platform, with only a few essentials.

 She stayed in the tree (named Luna) for more than two years. She didn't leave until the lumber company promised not to chop down Luna and the other trees.

 *The Simpsons* episode "Lisa the Tree Hugger" was inspired by Julia!

Imagine you are chosen to be a tree-sitter for two years. Up in the tree, you'll have a small mattress, a pillow, and blankets. Food will be provided. But what else will you need? Whatever you bring must fit in one backpack. Write a packing list of the items you cannot live without. And, remember, you won't have any cell phone service up there!

# JULIA CHILD

## CHEF

August 15, 1912–
August 13, 2004
United States

As an author and one of
the first women to host a
cooking show on TV, Julia
Child brought French cuisine
to millions of Americans
and taught a country that
cooking can be fun.

* Julia was rejected from military agencies during World War II because she was too tall. She was 6'2".

* She joined a spy agency, where one of her jobs was to make a repellent to keep sharks away from bombs that were planted on the ocean floor. Her concoction worked!

* Julia hosted TV shows where she showed audiences that cooking was part art and part science.

* She donated one of her famous TV kitchen sets to the Smithsonian Institution. It is on display in Washington, DC.

* One of her favorite dishes was French onion soup.

# JULIA LOPEZ
## painter
### Born January 1, 1936
### Mexico

Julia Lopez left her small village behind and became an artist. She used vivid colors to paint scenes from her childhood.

## ⚡SUPERPOWERS
### MEMORY, BRUSHWORK

* Julia worked alongside her seven sisters on her parents' farm. She was fascinated by the photos of places around the world that she saw at local fairs. She wanted to visit them.

* At 13, Julia ran away by hitching a ride on a coconut truck. Her older sister brought her home. It wasn't until she was 16 that Julia made it to Mexico City, where she became a maid.

* She met the famous painter Frida Kahlo, who got her a job posing for artists. Julia realized she wanted to paint too.

* She started painting on paper bags, creating landscapes and scenes from her childhood. Her artist friends refused to teach her. They loved her self-taught style!

# KAMALA HARRIS
## VICE PRESIDENT
### Born October 20, 1964
### United States

Kamala Harris is the first woman, first Black person, and first South Asian person to be vice president of the United States.

## SUPERPOWERS
### AMBITION, INTELLIGENCE

+ Kamala is the daughter of immigrants. Her father was born in Jamaica and her mother was born in India.

+ As a child, Kamala often went with her mother to civil rights demonstrations and marches.

+ Kamala was California's first Black senator and the country's first South Asian senator.

+ She ran for president before agreeing to be former Vice President Joe Biden's running mate.

+ Kamala loves wearing sneakers to work!

# KATERINA STEFANIDI

## POLE-VAULTER

Born February 4, 1990
Greece

Katerina Stefanidi is a high-flying pole-vaulter who doesn't allow her fears to stop her from reaching for the sky.

**SUPERPOWERS**
**AGILITY, CONSISTENCY**

+ At age 10, Katerina decided to become a pole-vaulter because it combined her love of running, jumping, and gymnastics.

+ Surpisingly, she is afraid of heights!

+ She won Olympic gold with a jump that sent her nearly 16 feet into the air.

+ Katerina sometimes has trouble traveling with her poles. They are 14 feet, 7 inches long. Some airlines won't take them!

# KATHERINE JOHNSON
## COMPUTER SCIENTIST
August 26, 1918–February 24, 2020
United States

Katherine Johnson overcame racial and gender bias to help astronauts reach for the stars (and then get back to Earth safely) with her incredible math skills.

When most kids her age were in the eighth grade, Katherine was already in high school. She started college when she was 15.

In 1961, Katherine was responsible for figuring out the path of the country's first human spaceflight.

Her work, along with the work of dozens of other Black women at NASA, went forgotten for years. The 2016 release of the movie *Hidden Figures* fixed that!

At age 97, Katherine received the Presidential Medal of Freedom from President Barack Obama.

**SUPERPOWER**
*PROBLEM-SOLVING*

# KATIA KRAFFT

## VOLCANOLOGIST

April 17, 1942–June 3, 1991
France

Katia Krafft and her husband, Maurice, tracked the world's most active and dangerous volcanoes for 25 years.

- At the age of 17, Katia saw a documentary about a volcanologist's attempts to get close to active eruptions. Right then, she knew what her life's work would be!

- Katia and Maurice took video and photos of volcanoes, as well as measurements and gas readings.

- Katia wore protective silver suits and helmets so she could withstand the heat from molten lava, which can be 1,300 to 2,200 degrees Fahrenheit. She invented a portable device that measures volcanic gases.

- Her most iconic item of clothing was a hat— a bright red beanie that she often wore out in the field.

# KEIKO FUKUDA
## JUDOKA
April 12, 1913–February 9, 2013
Japan and United States

**Five feet tall and less than 100 pounds, Keiko Fukuda proved one doesn't have to be big to succeed as a leading judo expert.**

 Growing up, Keiko was taught to do things that were considered appropriate for girls, like arranging flowers and performing tea ceremonies.

 Her mother thought judo would be a great way for Keiko to find a husband. Instead, Keiko rejected an arranged marriage and committed her life to judo.

* She learned judo from Jigoro Kano, who founded the martial art.

 At 98, she earned a tenth-degree black belt, becoming the first woman to earn this highest honor.

 Her personal motto was "Be strong, be gentle, be beautiful."

## SUPERPOWERS
### BALANCE, INDEPENDENCE

# KHERIS ROGERS

## FASHION DESIGNER

Born August 6, 2006
United States

Kheris Rogers was bullied because of her dark skin, so she started a fashion business that fights bullying.

⚡ **SUPERPOWERS** *SELF-LOVE, DRIVE*

✦ When Kheris was bullied for her dark skin, her sister Taylor reminded her what their grandma used to say: Flexin' in Her Complexion. The saying was meant to encourage the girls to love their skin tone.

✦ The two sisters put the saying on a T-shirt. They built a website, and the shirts sold out in 10 minutes!

✦ Kheris is the youngest designer to ever participate in New York's Harlem Fashion Week. She's also walked the runway in *America's Next Top Model*.

✦ Alicia Keys is one of her favorite singers.

# KIARA NIRGHIN
## SCIENTIST & INVENTOR

Born February 25, 2000
South Africa

Kiara Nirghin won the 2016 Google Science Fair with her method to increase food security in drought-stricken areas.

## SUPERPOWERS
### CURIOSITY, PERSEVERANCE

 Kiara made a material out of orange and avocado peels that could absorb lots of water.

She first came up with the idea for her invention at 13 years old, while she was in the hospital with bacterial meningitis.

 In 2016, Kiara was named one of *Time* magazine's 30 most influential teens.

She and poet Amanda Gorman once interviewed each other about the importance of STEAM education for girls.

# KIT DESLAURIERS

## SKI MOUNTAINEER

Born November 23, 1969
United States

While many adventurers dream of climbing the world's tallest mountains, Kit DesLauriers not only climbed them but also skied down each of them!

★ Kit is a world champion in free skiing, a sport that combines skiing with tricky acrobatic moves.

★ She's the first person to ski the Seven Summits, which are the highest mountain peaks on each continent. She is also the first woman to ski Mount Everest.

★ In 2015, *National Geographic* named Kit an adventurer of the year.

★ She leads expeditions into the Arctic National Wildlife Refuge to help measure the impact of climate change.

★ She raised a wolf pup named Alta!

## SUPERPOWERS
### ENDURANCE, FEARLESSNESS

# KOTCHAKORN VORAAKHOM

## — LANDSCAPE ARCHITECT —

### Born circa 1981
### Thailand

**Kotchakorn Voraakhom aims to keep sinking cities afloat with her parks, green spaces, and buildings that provide natural solutions to flooding.**

## ⚡SUPERPOWER *INNOVATION*

 Young Kotchakorn loved to play in the floodwaters and greenery that surrounded her house each rainy season.

 She submitted her idea for a park built on a slight angle to collect rainwater to a design competition—and won! The 11-acre park can collect more than 1 million gallons of rain.

 Her company designed and built Thailand's first green roof. There, visitors can learn to grow gardens in "wasted spaces," like roofs, using recycled water from buildings.

 In her spare time, Kotchakorn enjoys riding horses.

**Your Turn!**

Imagine you are a landscape architect like Kotchakorn and design a local park that solves a problem. For example, how can you keep slides from getting hot? Is there a way to prevent young kids from falling into a lake or fountain? Sketch the layout of your park on paper. To add some color, use watercolors or colored pencils.

# KRISTAL AMBROSE

## ENVIRONMENTAL SCIENTIST

Born December 7, 1989
The Bahamas

Kristal Ambrose fights to ban single-use plastic items to save our oceans.

+ While working at an aquarium, Kristal spent two days pulling plastic out of an injured sea turtle.

+ She created the Bahamas Plastic Movement, which develops solutions to plastic pollution.

+ Kristal drafted a bill that would outlaw single-use plastic items in the Bahamas. The bill passed, and today, if someone is caught importing or selling single-use plastics in the Bahamas, they could be fined thousands of dollars!

+ She often goes by the name Kristal Ocean.

# LADI KWALI

## POTTER

Circa 1925–
August 12, 1984
Nigeria

Born in a small village, Ladi Kwali achieved worldwide fame for her pottery, which she made using a combination of ancient and modern techniques.

- Ladi Kwali learned to make traditional pinched and coiled pots as a young girl.

- She adorned her pots with patterns featuring birds, fish, lizards, scorpions, and other animals.

- Her pots, cups, bowls, and vases appear in museums all around the world.

- Ladi Kwali is the first woman to appear on Nigerian currency, and major roads have been named after her.

- Her first name means "born on Sunday."

## SUPERPOWERS
### ARTISTRY, PRECISION

# LADY GAGA

## SINGER & ACTIVIST

Born March 28, 1986
United States

Superstar Lady Gaga uses her music, films, and even her clothes to spread messages of equality, kindness, and resilience.

**SUPERPOWERS** *COMPASSION, ORIGINALITY*

- Lady Gaga's real name is Stefani Joanne Angelina Germanotta.

- She once arrived at an awards show wearing a dress made completely out of meat. It weighed around 35 pounds!

- Lady Gaga is the first woman to win an Oscar, Grammy, BAFTA, and Golden Globe in the same year, all for her work on the soundtrack of the film *A Star Is Born*.

- She and her mom launched the Born This Way Foundation to help young people talk openly about mental illness.

# LAKSHMI BAI
## QUEEN & WARRIOR
November 19, 1828–June 18, 1858
India

Known as India's Warrior Queen, Lakshmi Bai battled the British army, who were trying to take her kingdom. She is celebrated as a hero of freedom.

**SUPERPOWER**
*COMBAT*

+ Lakshmi could read and write, which was rare for Indian women at the time. She also trained in martial arts, horseback riding, archery, sword fighting, weightlifting, and wrestling.

+ She created an army that had both men and women.

+ After trying to negotiate a settlement over her kingdom, she and her army fought the British. Her army was overcome, but Lakshmi escaped on horseback with her adopted son tied to her back.

+ Today, young girls in India dress up like Lakshmi. The costume usually includes a bright-colored sari, a headscarf, and a sword.

# LASKARINA "BOUBOULINA" PINOTSIS

## NAVAL COMMANDER

Circa May 1771–
May 22, 1825
Turkey and Greece

Laskarina "Bouboulina" Pinotsis fought for independence with her own fleet of ships, which she commanded.

* When her second husband, a rich merchant, died, Laskarina took over his ships and his business. She grew her fortune—while secretly working for Greek independence.

* Laskarina built a giant warship with 18 cannons and called it the *Agamemnon*, after an ancient Greek king.

* Her fleet of ships went into battle against the Ottoman Empire. She captured fortresses and saved many Greek towns from destruction.

* She died a few years before her dream of an independent Greece came true. She was given the honorary rank of admiral—the first woman in the world to hold this title.

* A statue of her stands on the island of Spetses.

# LAUREN POTTER

## actor

Born May 10, 1990
United States

Lauren Potter was denied a spot on her high school's cheerleading squad, but that didn't stop her from auditioning—and getting cast—to play a cheerleader on TV.

* Lauren was born with Down syndrome, which can delay how a child develops. She didn't walk until she was two years old.

* Lauren shot to fame when she got the role of Becky on the hit show *Glee*.

* President Obama appointed her to the Presidential Committee for People with Intellectual Disabilities. She also served as an ambassador for the Special Olympics World Games.

* She travels across the country speaking about her experience fighting against bullying.

* Her favorite breakfast is eggs, bacon, and toast.

**SUPERPOWERS**

HUMOR, EMPATHY

# LEAH CHASE
## CHEF

January 6, 1923–
June 1, 2019
United States

**Known as the Queen of Creole Cuisine, Leah Chase fed presidents, civil rights leaders, Supreme Court justices, artists, and musicians for nearly half a century!**

⭐ Leah was Creole, which is a term referring to Louisiana's multiracial population—French, Spanish, African, and Native American.

⭐ She got started in the restaurant business when she went to work with her husband, Dooky Chase, at his dad's restaurant. Leah became the restaurant's head chef when she realized it didn't have one.

## ⚡SUPERPOWERS
### *COMMUNITY BUILDING, rICH FLAVORS*

⭐ The restaurant became a meeting place for civil rights leaders, including Martin Luther King Jr. and his father, who loved her barbecued ribs.

⭐ Princess Tiana, the waitress who wanted to own a restaurant in the movie *The Princess and the Frog*, was based on Leah!

# LELLA LOMBARDI
## FORMULA ONE RACER
### March 26, 1941–March 3, 1992
### Italy

Lella Lombardi proved that she could speed past the competition in a male-dominated sport.

✦ Lella learned to drive by helping her father deliver meat in his van. Her father would time how long it took her to get around town.

✦ At the age of 18, Lella bought a used race car and started racing professionally. She quickly moved up the ranks.

✦ Lella was the second woman to compete in a Formula One race and the first woman to compete in the US Grand Prix.

✦ After her Formula One career, Lella won several endurance races. These are car races that last up to six hours.

# LÉOPOLDINE DOUALLA-BELL SMITH

## FLIGHT ATTENDANT

### Born 1939
### Cameroon

This princess was born to fly! Léopoldine Doualla-Bell Smith was the first Black flight attendant in the world.

* Léopoldine was a princess of the Royal Douala family of Cameroon.

* She was sent to Paris for training as a flight attendant. During her first assignment at the age of 17, she panicked. She had never been on a flight before!

* From witnessing apartheid in South Africa to the racial divide in the US, Léopoldine had a front-row seat to how Black people were treated in different countries.

* Her husband gave her the nickname Double Oh One because her employee card read 001.

* Even after retiring, Léopoldine would volunteer at the Denver International Airport, welcoming visitors and helping them find their way around the airport.

SUPERPOWER KINDNESS

# LEYMAH GBOWEE

## PEACE ACTIVIST

### Born February 1, 1972
### Liberia

Leymah Gbowee helped stop her country's long-lasting civil war by bringing women together to call for peace.

**SUPERPOWER** *INSTIGATION*

* Leymah's childhood dreams of becoming a doctor were crushed when a civil war broke out in her country just as she graduated from high school.

* She became the leader of the Women in Peacebuilding Network and recruited women from many different backgrounds to protest the war. They led demonstrations, sit-ins, and rallies.

* Her movement helped to elect Ellen Johnson Sirleaf as president of Liberia—the first woman elected to be head of an African country.

* Leymah won the Nobel Peace Prize for her amazing efforts to end the war.

# LILIAN BLAND

## aviator

September 22, 1878–
May 11, 1971
United Kingdom

In an age when many people believed women were supposed to run a household, Lilian Bland took to the skies!

## ⚡SUPERPOWERS *INNOVATION, BOLDNESS*

❋ Lilian lived an unconventional life. She worked as a photographer, wore men's trousers, loved hunting and fishing, taught martial arts classes, and more.

❋ After receiving a postcard from her uncle that showed a picture of aviator Louis Blériot, Lilian decided to build her own airplane.

❋ She added an engine to her glider, which became the first motorized aircraft in Ireland. She called her airplane the *Mayfly*.

❋ Lilian was the first woman to design, build, and fly her own airplane.

❋ Her father promised her a Model T Ford automobile if she stopped her dangerous hobby. She agreed and opened the first car dealership in Ireland!

# LINA BO BARDI
## architect
December 5, 1914–
March 20, 1992
Italy and Brazil

**Lina Bo Bardi designed many important buildings in Brazil, including theaters, cultural centers, and the São Paulo Museum of Art.**

- Lina opened her own architecture studio in Milan, Italy. Sadly, it was destroyed during World War II.

- Her first masterpiece was the home she built for herself in Brazil, which she called Casa de Vidro, or the Glass House. It is a large glass box suspended above the ground.

- When drawing buildings, Lina liked to use a variety of tools, such as pens, watercolors, and brushes.

- She created a big, round chair known as Bardi's Bowl.

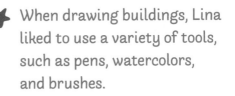

SUPERPOWER
creativity

# LISA LESLIE

## BASKETBALL PLAYER

Born July 7, 1972
United States

A four-time Olympic gold medalist, Lisa Leslie was a star player in the WNBA. She was named MVP three times and All Star seven times.

### ⚡ SUPERPOWERS

*AGILITY, AMAZING AIM*

⭐ By the time she was in second grade, Lisa was already taller than her teacher.

⭐ In high school, Lisa once scored 101 points in 16 minutes! The other team refused to play the second half of the game.

⭐ Lisa was one of the first athletes to play for the Women's National Basketball Association (WNBA). She was the first player to dunk in a WNBA game.

⭐ Lisa wants to lead the next generation of young people in basketball with the Lisa Leslie Basketball & Leadership Academy.

⭐ She used to want to be a weather reporter.

# LIZ CLAIBORNE
## FASHION DESIGNER & CEO

March 31, 1929–June 26, 2007
Belgium and United States

Liz Claiborne believed that women's professional clothing should be affordable, comfortable, and stylish.

⭐ Liz's fashion label was the first company founded by a woman to make the Fortune 500—a list of the highest-earning companies in the US.

⭐ Her father loved art. He wanted Liz to be a painter like him, but she had her heart set on making clothes.

⭐ Liz cut her hair short after getting her first job in fashion. She said this was how she declared her independence from her parents.

⭐ In 1991, Liz was inducted into the National Sales Hall of Fame.

**SUPERPOWERS**
AMBITION, ARTISTIC VISION

# LOKI SCHMIDT

## CONSERVATIONIST

March 3, 1919–
October 21, 2010
Germany

Loki Schmidt worked to protect the Earth's endangered plant species. She also spread awareness about the importance of biodiversity.

⭐ Loki grew up visiting the botanical garden in her city. There she fell in love with flowers and conservationism.

⭐ While her husband served as the chancellor of Germany, Loki used her influence to start a Flower of the Year Award to celebrate Germany's endangered wildflowers.

⭐ On a trip to Mexico, she discovered a new species of pineapple: the *Pitcairnia loki-schmidtii*.

⭐ Loki's classmates called her Schmeling, after a famous boxer, because she wasn't afraid to step in and defend other kids from bullies on the playground.

# LORELLA PRAELI
## IMMIGRATION ACTIVIST
### Born August 18, 1988
### Peru and United States

Using her voice to create change, Lorella Praeli has devoted her life to immigration reform.

**⚡SUPERPOWER** *resilience*

⭐ When Lorella was 10, she moved from Peru to Connecticut as an undocumented child. She was at risk of being sent back to Peru, but she was determined to make a new home in the US.

⭐ Growing up, Lorella faced bullying in school because she had only one leg.

⭐ She started an organization that helps undocumented students like her go to college.

⭐ Lorella has a cocker spaniel named Simba.

⭐ A song she listens to on repeat is "Eye of the Tiger" by Survivor.

# LORENA OCHOA

## GOLFER

Born November 15, 1981
Mexico

Lorena Ochoa is a record-setting golfer whose skill and fearlessness on the golf course earned her the nickname *La Tigresa*, or the Tiger.

★ When Lorena was five years old, she'd help steer her dad's golf cart around the course near their house and watch him play.

★ Before her games, Lorena would visit the golf course groundskeepers to thank them for their work and make them breakfast.

★ She helped start La Barranca, a school for underprivileged elementary and high school students in her hometown of Guadalajara. Since the school opened, more than 6,000 students have graduated from it!

★ Lorena is the second-youngest professional golfer to be honored in the World Golf Hall of Fame.

★ One of her favorite foods is Nutella.

**SUPERPOWERS** *DEDICATION, PRECISION*

# LOWRI MORGAN
## ULTRAMARATHON RUNNER
### Born 1975
### United Kingdom

Lowri Morgan is an extreme sports athlete who participates in thrill-seeking adventures.

## SUPERPOWER *ENDURANCE*

+ Before she found her love for athletics, Lowri wanted to be a professional singer.

+ When she was 19, she injured herself so badly that doctors said she would never run again.

+ Lowri ran an ultramarathon in the Arctic, one of the coldest places on Earth. That year, she was the only person to reach the finish line.

+ Every morning, she wakes up at 4:30 a.m. to go running with her dog Nel and train for her next marathon. She runs more than 30 miles a week!

+ Lowri enjoys making documentaries.

# LUCIE PINSON

## CLIMATE ACTIVIST

Born November 4, 1985
France

**Lucie Pinson is an environmentalist who pressures banks and insurers to stop working with coal companies.**

 **SUPERPOWER** *PERSUASION*

 Lucie first learned about the dangers of coal production when she traveled to South Africa for school. As soon as she returned to France, she took action.

 Using the press, social media, protests, letter-writing, and persistent campaigning, she convinced more than 20 banks and 17 insurers to stop working with coal companies.

* Lucie can't choose her favorite color: it's between red and green!

* She loves eating raw carrots and doing puzzles.

YOUR TURN!

Lucie won the 2020 Goldman Environmental Prize, which awarded her $200,000 to continue her advocacy work. If you were to create an award, what would it be called? Who would you give it to and why? What could the prize be used for?

# LUCY KING
## ZOOLOGIST
Born October 30, 1977
United Kingdom and Kenya

Lucy King learned that elephants are afraid of bees, so she devised a beehive fence to keep elephants from farmers' crops.

* Lucy grew up in Somalia, Lesotho, and Kenya.

* During her childhood, she spent a lot of her time in national parks all over Africa.

* One hot day, Lucy witnessed elephants moving away from a swarm of bees. She realized that the sound of buzzing bees might be used to keep elephants out of certain areas.

* The beehive fence she designed keeps up to 80% of elephants away from farms.

* Chocolate is one of her greatest motivators.

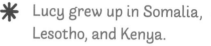

SUPERPOWER CURIOSITY

# LUO DENGPING

## EXTREME ROCK CLIMBER

Born 1980
China

**Luo Dengping is an expert rock climber. She is her village's very own Spider-Woman.**

* Growing up in China, Luo watched her father and the other men in her village climb up high cliffs without ropes, harnesses, nets, or any safety equipment to gather herbs and swallow droppings for medicine and fertilizer.

* When Luo turned 15, she decided to try free-climbing.

* She wanted a professional to train her, but no one would. With her father's help, Luo was soon able to climb just as fast as the male climbers.

* She and other climbers perform courageous feats to entertain tourists. Twice a day, they climb 328 feet up and down cliffs. That's the equivalent of a 30-story building!

* Luo is the first woman in her village's history to continue the rock climbing tradition.

# LUPITA NYONG'O

## actor

Born March 1, 1983
Mexico, Kenya,
and United States

Lupita Nyong'o is an award-winning actor, children's book author, and champion for diversity and representation in the arts.

Lupita was born in Mexico City after her family fled unrest and danger in Kenya.

Her name was chosen in honor of the place she was born. Her parents named her after Mexico's Virgin of Guadalupe—Lupita for short.

She is the first Mexican-born and Kenyan actor to receive an Academy Award.

Lupita wrote a picture book called *Sulwe* about a young Black girl who learns to love her dark complexion.

Before attending any red carpet event, she makes sure to have a plate of one of her favorite foods: steak tacos.

# MADAM C. J. WALKER
## entrepreneur
### December 23, 1867–May 25, 1919
### United States

The first self-made woman millionaire in the United States, Madam C. J. Walker employed thousands of Black women in her hair care business.

- Madam was the first person in her family to be born free after the Emancipation Proclamation.

- Madam claimed that the formula for her famous Madam Walker's Wonder Hair Grower was revealed to her in a dream.

- During her lifetime, she was one of the major donors to the National Association for the Advancement of Colored People (NAACP).

- Her home, Villa Lewaro, in Irvington, New York, became a notable meeting place during the Harlem Renaissance. Visitors included writers and thinkers, like Langston Hughes, W. E. B. Du Bois, and Zora Neale Hurston.

# MADAME SAQUI

## acrobat

February 26, 1786–
January 21, 1866
France

Madame Saqui was a renowned acrobat, rope dancer, and tightrope walker whose skills and feats made her known as the Darling of Paris.

+ Before Madame Saqui became known by her stage name, she was called Marguerite. Her father was once a circus performer and an acrobat, but he hoped she would follow the family business selling natural remedies.

+ Marguerite convinced one of her father's circus friends to teach her how to walk across a tightrope. She nailed her first public performance at the age of 11.

+ Abandoning the medicine business, Marguerite's family began touring with her as a circus group.

+ Marguerite adopted her stage name when she married fellow acrobat Julian Saqui.

+ French emperor Napoleon Bonaparte thought she was incredible!

+ She walked the tightrope for one final performance when she turned 60.

**SUPERPOWER** *BALANCE*

# MADELEINE ALBRIGHT

## POLITICIAN & DIPLOMAT

May 15, 1937–
March 23, 2022
Czech Republic
and United States

Madeleine Albright was determined to make positive changes for refugees and fight for the country that gave her a second home.

+ Madeleine fled Czechoslovakia (now the Czech Republic) with her family when she was nine years old after it was invaded by the Nazis during World War II. The family eventually settled in Colorado.

+ Madeleine was nominated to be secretary of state by then-president Bill Clinton.

+ She was the first female secretary of state in US history. She was also the highest-ranking woman in the entire government.

+ Madeleine loved keeping up with physical fitness. In 2006, she claimed that she could leg press 400 pounds—at almost 70 years old!

**SUPERPOWERS**
**INTELLIGENCE, CONVICTION**

# MADONNA

## SINGER, SONGWRITER, & BUSINESSWOMAN

Born August 16, 1958
United States

Madonna is a groundbreaking triple-threat entertainer known as the Queen of Pop.

As a kid, Madonna loved to perform for her classmates. Often, she'd do cartwheels and handstands in the school hallways.

When she was 20, Madonna left home with just $35 in her pocket to start her career in New York City.

She's broken 16 Guinness World Records!

There is an animal species named after her. It's a type of tardigrade, or water bear, called *Echiniscus madonnae*.

**SUPERPOWERS**

## allure, fierceness

# MAE C. JEMISON
## astronaut & Doctor
### Born October 17, 1956
### United States

A multitalented scientist, Mae C. Jemison was the first Black woman to go to space.

As a girl, Mae tried all sorts of activities: sewing dresses, learning different styles of dance, and fixing broken toys.

She didn't know if she wanted to be a fashion designer, an astronaut, a dancer, or an engineer.

When she was young, Mae watched the TV show *Star Trek* and saw Nyota Uhura, a Black space lieutenant. It made her want to go to space too. In 1993, Mae made a guest appearance on the show.

Mae often danced in space. Because there was little gravity, she could do leg lifts, leap around the shuttle, and spin around 10 times with ease!

# MALALA YOUSAFZAI

## — EDUCATION ACTIVIST —

Born July 12, 1997
Pakistan and United Kingdom

**Malala Yousafzai spoke out against the Taliban,
a religious and political organization that
prevented girls from going to school.**

## SUPERPOWERS *courage, resilience*

 Malala's father was a schoolteacher and ran a
girls' school in their village.

 When Malala criticized the Taliban on her blog, she
wrote under the pen name "Gul Makai."

 In 2014, she was awarded the Nobel Peace Prize.
At the age of 17, Malala was the youngest person
to ever win the award!

* She is a huge fan of the TV show *Friends*.

* There is an asteroid named after her.

Malala wrote a blog about her life as a young girl under Taliban rule. Everyone has a story to tell. Think about a challenge in your life or something that is important to you. What could you blog about? Who do you want to read it? Write an entry and see where it goes!

# MALIKA OUFKIR
## author

Born April 2, 1953
Morocco and France

Malika Oufkir is a courageous writer and activist whose childhood experiences made her an advocate for the just treatment of prisoners.

**SUPERPOWERS**
**DETERMINATION, PATIENCE**

* Malika grew up in the palace of Morocco's king. While she was able to ride horses, play, and spend time with others, she missed her family.

* At 15, Malika returned to her family. She shopped with her mother in Paris, danced to disco music, and had fun with friends. Life changed when her father tried to overthrow the king. Her father died, and the rest of her family was imprisoned.

* After years in captivity, Malika and her siblings devised a plan to escape using spoons and the sharp lid of a sardine can.

* Malika wrote about her prison experience in a book called *Stolen Lives: Twenty Years in a Desert Jail.*

# MANAL AL-SHARIF

## COMPUTER SCIENTIST & WOMEN'S RIGHTS ACTIVIST

Born April 25, 1979
Saudi Arabia, United Arab
Emirates, and Australia

Manal al-Sharif campaigned to earn women the right to drive in her home country of Saudi Arabia.

+ Manal's country forbade women from doing many things without a man's permission, like driving, going to school, or taking "unladylike" jobs.

+ She worked as an IT security specialist for an oil company. She was the only woman at her job.

+ Manal filmed herself driving her brother's car so other women would see it and be inspired to speak up. She was arrested many times, but she never gave up.

+ Because of Manal and dozens of other women who defied the driving rules, Saudi Arabia reversed the driving ban for women in 2018!

**SUPERPOWERS**
DEFIANCE, ORGANIZATION

# MARGARET ATWOOD

## AUTHOR

Born November 18, 1939
Canada

Margaret Atwood's riveting stories have captured the attention of readers around the world.

## ⚡SUPERPOWERS
### WIT, IMAGINATION

⭐ Growing up in the forests of northern Canada with her family, Margaret loved reading mysteries, comic books, and stories like *Grimms' Fairy Tales*. When she turned six, she started writing plays and poems of her own.

⭐ Margaret published her first book of poetry when she was 22. She did everything herself, from drawing the cover to printing the pages. Even though she made only a few hundred copies, the book won an award and encouraged her to keep writing.

⭐ Margaret's famous novel *The Handmaid's Tale* sold millions of copies. The story was turned into an opera, a movie, a TV series, a play, and even a ballet.

⭐ She invented an electronic pen so she can sign books remotely.

# MARGARET HAMILTON

## COMPUTER SCIENTIST

Born August 17, 1936
United States

As a computer scientist for NASA, Margaret Hamilton wrote the software responsible for safely landing astronauts on the moon.

## ⚡SUPERPOWERS
### CLEVERNESS, CALCULATION

✳ After graduating from college, Margaret took a job writing software that predicted the weather.

✳ She often brought her young daughter to work. While she wrote code, little Lauren took naps in the office.

✳ The computers Margaret programmed were the size of entire rooms! Instead of typing on a keyboard or clicking a screen, she wrote code on paper punch cards.

✳ Just as the *Apollo 11* astronauts were about to land on the moon, NASA's team on Earth started getting error messages. Because Margaret's software was able to recognize that the errors weren't serious, she saved the moon landing!

# MARGARET ZHANG
## FASHION STYLIST & EDITOR
### Born May 27, 1993
### China and Australia

In 2021, Margaret Zhang became the youngest editor in chief of the magazine *Vogue China*.

 **SUPERPOWER** *CREATIVITY*

⭐ Growing up, Margaret danced ballet, played piano, and made her own clothes.

⭐ She began her career in fashion as a blogger. She started her blog *Shine by Three* when she was 16.

⭐ Margaret enjoys filmmaking. She's directed her own short films, including one inspired by her musical upbringing.

⭐ She loves to dye her hair fun colors like hot pink and turquoise!

# MARGHERITA HACK

## ASTROPHYSICIST

June 12, 1922–
June 29, 2013
Italy

**Margherita Hack traveled the world giving lectures and interviews about astrophysics. By using plain language, she helped make the subject accessible to millions of people.**

* Margherita was the first woman director of an astronomical observatory in Italy.

* In addition to her work as a scientist, she was an activist who championed women's and gay rights.

* She loved animals. She was a vegetarian for most of her life, and she cared for many pets.

* A free spirit, Margherita wore an inside-out overcoat at her wedding.

* In 1995, the asteroid 8558 Hack was named in her honor.

# MARIA CALLAS
## opera singer
December 2, 1923–September 16, 1977
United States and Greece

**Maria Callas's soprano voice and stage presence earned her the nickname *La Divina*, or the Divine One.**

**SUPERPOWER** *MESMERIZING VOCALS*

* Maria was the youngest of three sisters. Her mother encouraged her to sing in public to help the family earn money.

* After receiving formal training from several music teachers in Greece, Maria played roles in more than a dozen operas. She gave hundreds of performances all around the world.

* Maria taught voice lessons to aspiring young singers who hoped to follow in her footsteps.

* Her poodles, Djedda, Pixie, and Toy, were her constant companions.

Maria was incredibly talented. She honed her singing skills by practicing rich, low notes and sweet, high notes—and everything in between. Spend just five minutes trying all the different notes you can sing. How high or low can you go? Don't be afraid to sing as loud as you can!

# MARIA GOEPPERT MAYER

## THEORETICAL PHYSICIST

June 28, 1906–February 20, 1972
Poland and United States

Maria Goeppert Mayer's research into the nucleus of atoms made her the second female Nobel Prize winner in physics.

**SUPERPOWER**

**INTELLIGENCE**

- Maria is the seventh generation of professors on her father's side of the family.

- She spent a lot of her career doing research in empty rooms and labs at the universities that employed her husband. None of these universities wanted to pay Maria to be a professor, even though she was qualified.

- Maria didn't get a full-time, paid teaching position at a university until she'd been working as a physicist for 30 years.

- Her research explored why some atoms have a more stable nucleus than others.

- The Goeppert-Mayer crater on Venus is named after her.

# MARÍA ISABEL URRUTIA

## WEIGHTLIFTER

Born March 25, 1965
Colombia

María Isabel Urrutia was the first woman in South America to win an individual gold medal in the Olympics.

✦ María began her career as an athlete competing in shot put and discus.

✦ In her first major weightlifting competition, she wowed onlookers and her fellow athletes by placing second.

✦ After retiring from athletics, she was elected to the Chamber of Representatives of Colombia twice!

✦ She wants to make sure athletes like her are supported and rewarded by the government.

✦ The character of Luisa Madrigal in the film *Encanto* was inspired by María!

# MARIA MONTESSORI
## PHYSICIAN & EDUCATOR
August 31, 1870–May 6, 1952
Italy

Maria Montessori revolutionized early childhood education. The Montessori Method she developed is used in thousands of schools around the world today.

- Maria believed that hands-on activity was an important part of early childhood education. She wanted kids to play, experiment, and discover, instead of being told what to do.

- In addition to being an educator, Maria was the first female physician in Italy!

- She was a dedicated feminist.

- Before becoming a doctor, Maria studied mathematics.

- She developed her curriculum by working with children with disabilities.

**SUPERPOWERS** NURTURING, PLAYFULNESS

# MARIA REICHE

## archeologist

May 15, 1903–
June 8, 1998
Germany and Peru

Maria Reiche dedicated herself to researching the Nazca Lines in Peru. The mysterious lines etched into the earth make enormous patterns and images.

+ Maria originally left Germany for Peru to teach at a German language school. When she discovered the Nazca Lines, she dedicated the rest of her life to studying and protecting them.

+ While performing her archeological research, Maria lived in a hut she built herself in the desert. She lived there without any electricity or running water for 40 years!

+ Her commitment earned her the nickname the Lady of the Lines.

## SUPERPOWER
### INQUISITIVENESS

+ The people in Nazca didn't realize that Maria was an archeologist at first. They thought she might be a witch. Eventually, they left food out for her when they saw her working in the field.

# MARIA SIBYLLA MERIAN

## Naturalist

April 2, 1647–
January 13, 1717
Germany and the Netherlands

**Maria Sibylla Merian created detailed and accurate illustrations of moths and butterflies, which educated other naturalists and the public about metamorphosis.**

✳ Maria's stepfather painted flowers and still lifes. He encouraged her to pick up a paintbrush.

✳ When Maria was 13, she raised silkworms in jars. Every day, she'd watch her silkworms grow and change as she recorded the stages of their life cycle.

✳ For a long time, people thought butterflies sprouted magically out of mud. Maria's observations helped prove that they developed from caterpillars.

✳ She wrote a book in Latin about her research. It included 60 scientific copperplate engravings.

**SUPERPOWERS**
*CURIOSITY,
DRAWING SKILLS*

# MARIANA PAJÓN

## BMX CYCLIST
Born October 10, 1991
Colombia

Mariana Pajón won a national title at age five and a world title at age nine. Her many championship wins earned her the nickname Queen of BMX.

**SUPERPOWERS** CONSISTENCY, SUPER SPEED

When Mariana won her world title at age nine, she was the only girl who competed in the race.

She is the first Colombian athlete to win an Olympic gold medal twice.

If she weren't cycling, Mariana has said she would want to study medicine.

She accidentally wore one white glove and one black glove when she won the World Championships. Now, she makes sure to always wear mismatched racing gloves!

# MARIE CURIE

## SCIENTIST

November 7, 1867–
July 4, 1934
Poland and France

For her work studying radioactivity, Marie Curie became the first woman to be awarded a Nobel Prize. She would eventually win a second one!

## SUPERPOWERS
### INTELLIGENCE, CONVICTION

When Marie was a teenager, she agreed to work as a governess and tutor to pay for her sister Bronya to go to medical school. Later, Bronya got a job and paid Marie's way through school.

Through her research, she uncovered two new radioactive metals: polonium and radium.

During World War II, she and her daughter Irène led a team of women driving and operating *Petites Curies*, cars with X-ray equipment in them. They helped treat thousands of wounded Allied troops on the battlefield.

Marie's scientific equipment and notebooks are still radioactive today!

# MARINA ABRAMOVIĆ

## PERFORMANCE ARTIST

### Born November 30, 1946
### Serbia

Performance artist Marina Abramović tests her own physical and psychological limits in her artwork.

**⚡SUPERPOWERS**
*SELF-CONTROL, ORIGINALITY*

★ Before exploring performance art, Marina studied painting.

★ During her performance at the Museum of Modern Art in New York City, *The Artist Is Present*, Marina sat still in a chair eight hours a day for several weeks. If visitors were silent and still, they were allowed to sit in a chair opposite her for as long as they liked.

★ In less than three months, *The Artist Is Present* attracted a record-breaking 850,000 visitors.

★ In one of her performances, Marina and her partner started at opposite ends of the Great Wall of China. They walked until they met in the middle to say goodbye and end their relationship.

# MARJANE SATRAPI

## GRAPHIC NOVELIST

Born November 22, 1969
Iran and France

**Marjane Satrapi is an artist who grew up in Iran. She is best known for writing and illustrating a graphic novel that tells her story of living through the Iranian Revolution.**

**SUPERPOWERS** *DEFIANCE, STORYTELLING*

 Marjane and her family lived under a government that told the Iranian people, especially women, what they could and couldn't do.

 Marjane did not grow up with any toys, but her house was full of books that sparked her imagination.

 Her graphic novel *Persepolis* was adapted into an animated film that was nominated for an Academy Award.

 When she was young, she said she wanted to be a bank robber—until she found out she could be arrested for it!

Marjane's book *Persepolis* was based on her own childhood. The story is told in black-and-white comic panels. Try drawing a few panels of a comic book based on your own life. What scenes would be important? What characters would you include? What colors would you use? Bring your story to life on the page.

YOUR TURN!

# MARSAI MARTIN

## actor & executive producer

Born August 21, 2004
United States

At the age of 13, Marsai became the youngest executive producer of a Hollywood film.

SUPERPOWER
CONFIDENCE

- When Marsai was nine years old, her family moved to Los Angeles from Texas to help her pursue her acting dreams.

- Less than a year after arriving in Los Angeles, Marsai landed a major role in the hit TV show *Black-ish*.

- In 2018, she made *Time* magazine's list of the most influential teens.

- *Little*—the film that she pitched, executive produced, and starred in—grossed $48 million worldwide.

- When Marsai is feeling stressed, she writes in her journal, relaxes in the bath, listens to music, or talks out her troubles with her grandmother.

# MARSHA P. JOHNSON

## LGBTQIA+ ACTIVIST

August 24, 1945–
July 6, 1992
United States

Often called Queen or Saint, Marsha P. Johnson was committed to the safety of gay and trans youth.

### SUPERPOWERS
GLAMOUR, EMPATHY

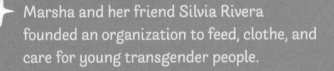

+ Marsha and her friend Silvia Rivera founded an organization to feed, clothe, and care for young transgender people.

+ In addition to her activism and community organizing, Marsha modeled for the artist Andy Warhol.

+ She loved wearing sequins and glitter, and would sometimes put fake fruit and flowers in her hair.

+ Marsha was a member of a touring drag performance troupe called Hot Peaches.

+ She said that the *P* in her name stood for her motto, "Pay it no mind!"

# MARTA VIEIRA DA SILVA
## soccer player
### Born February 19, 1986
### Brazil and Sweden

**Marta Vieira da Silva is considered the greatest woman soccer player in history. She has been named the World Player of the Year six times.**

**SUPERPOWERS** *SPEED, FANCY FOOTWORK*

+ When Marta was little, her mother couldn't afford to send her to school. So Marta helped support her family by selling fruit at the market. In her free time, she played soccer with the boys in her neighborhood.

+ While playing soccer in Sweden, Marta taught herself fluent Swedish by watching television! She now holds dual citizenship in Brazil and Sweden.

+ Marta led the Brazilian national soccer team to win two silver medals at the Olympics.

+ As a UN Women Goodwill Ambassador, she fights for gender equality in sports.

+ She has three dogs: Zoe, Zeca, and Toby!

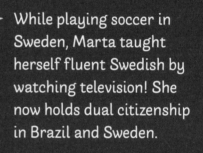

# MARY ANNING
## PALEONTOLOGIST
May 21, 1799–March 9, 1847
United Kingdom

Mary Anning discovered and identified many complete ancient skeletons. Her fossils changed how people understood the history of life on Earth.

**SUPERPOWER** *CURIOSITY*

Mary lived in a part of England nicknamed the Jurassic Coast. There are limestone cliffs there full of fossils from the Jurassic period.

Her whole family collected fossils and often sold them to support themselves.

During the 1800s, many people believed that Earth was only a few thousand years old. Mary's discoveries helped convince people that there had been life on Earth for hundreds of millions of years!

Mary uncovered the first full skeleton of a plesiosaur—a giant marine reptile that lived many millions of years ago.

# MARY EDWARDS WALKER

## SURGEON

November 26, 1832–
February 21, 1919
United States

Mary Edwards Walker was the first woman US Army surgeon. After serving the Union in the American Civil War, she dedicated the rest of her life to women's rights.

* Mary's parents believed that girls should be educated and that they shouldn't have to wear stuffy corsets and skirts.

* Mary was one of the first women to graduate from medical school in the US.

* For her work treating wounded Union soldiers during the Civil War, she became the first woman to be awarded the Medal of Honor.

* Mary preferred to wear pants and wore them all her life—including at her wedding!

* She tried running for office twice. Even though she wasn't elected, she used her platform to campaign for women's right to vote.

# MARY KINGSLEY

## explorer

October 13, 1862–June 3, 1900
United Kingdom

Through her travel writings, Mary Kingsley educated Europeans about West African plants and animals and challenged racist stereotypes.

* Even though Mary wasn't allowed to attend school, her father made sure she learned German so she could translate scientific books for him.

* Mary traveled to West Africa to study African religions and law, but she fell in love with the land and decided to become an explorer.

* She collected many examples of West African freshwater fish and beetles to bring back to the British Museum.

* Of all her accomplishments, Mary was especially proud of her ability to paddle a canoe.

**SUPERPOWER**
*ADVENTUROUSNESS*

# MARY SHELLEY

## author

August 30, 1797–
February 1, 1851
United Kingdom

---

At a ghost story competition with her friends, Mary came up with *Frankenstein*, one of the most beloved horror stories of all time.

**SUPERPOWER**

**IMAGINATION**

⭐ Mary's mother, Mary Wollstonecraft, was a celebrated feminist philosopher.

⭐ Mary was 21 when her first novel, *Frankenstein*, was published. She originally published it anonymously.

⭐ Even though she wrote one of the most famous stories in history, Mary never earned any royalties from the book.

⭐ Today, *Frankenstein* is considered one of the earliest examples of science fiction.

# MARYAM MIRZAKHANI

## MATHEMATICIAN

May 3, 1977–July 14, 2017
Iran and United States

Maryam Mirzakhani studied the geometry of unusual surfaces. She became the first woman and first Iranian to win the Fields Medal, the most prestigious prize in mathematics.

**SUPERPOWER**

**CALCULATION**

⭐ As a child, Maryam loved to read and dreamed about becoming a writer.

⭐ In high school, she competed in the International Mathematical Olympiad—and won the gold medal twice in a row!

⭐ Maryam liked to do math on large pieces of paper that she spread out on the floor.

⭐ Her work with the geometry of complex surfaces is being used in all sorts of fields. Some scientists use her work to study how the universe came to exist.

# MATILDE MONTOYA

## DOCTOR

March 14, 1859–
January 26, 1939
Mexico

**Fighting against a medical system that wanted to keep women out, Matilde Montoya became Mexico's first female doctor.**

* A quick learner, Matilde entered high school when she was just 12 years old.

* The National School of Medicine tried hard to expel her from their doctoral program because she was a woman. Matilde wrote directly to the president of Mexico, sharing her story. He agreed that she had the right to study, and she was let back into the university.

* The president of Mexico personally oversaw Matilde's final exam and attended her medical school graduation.

* Matilde was committed to gender equality in medicine. She helped found an organization called the Mexican Association of Female Doctors.

## SUPERPOWERS
### INTELLIGENCE, DEDICATION

# MAUD STEVENS WAGNER

## TATTOO ARTIST

February, 1877–
January 30, 1961
United States

Maud Stevens Wagner was the first known female tattoo artist in the United States.

## SUPERPOWERS UNIQUENESS, ARTISTRY

* Maud performed as an aerialist and contortionist in the circus.

* She learned how to tattoo from another circus performer, Gus Wagner. They eventually got married.

* Maud had all sorts of designs tattooed on her body: butterflies, lions, horses, monkeys, snakes, trees, and more!

* She and Gus taught their daughter Lovetta how to tattoo when she was nine years old.

# MAYA ANGELOU
## author
April 4, 1928–May 28, 2014
United States

**Maya Angelou was a legendary poet and memoirist whose brave storytelling made her one of the most celebrated writers in history.**

✳ Maya was often afraid to speak aloud when she was a child. She quietly memorized the words she heard around her: poems, lyrics, family stories, and conversations.

✳ Before she became a writer, Maya worked as a fry cook, tram attendant, civil rights activist, journalist, actor, singer, dancer, playwright, director, and producer.

✳ Maya liked to wake up early, go to a nearby hotel, and write in bed. She would pour her thoughts onto yellow legal pads and often finish 10 to 12 pages before returning home in the afternoon.

✳ In 2022, she became the first Black woman to be featured on the back of a US quarter.

# MAYA GABEIRA
## surfer
### Born April 10, 1987
### Brazil

**A risk taker, Maya Gabeira has broken world records with nothing but her surfboard.**

⭐ Maya started surfing when she was 14 years old. She wanted to find the biggest waves possible.

⭐ She broke the Guinness World Record for surfing a 73-foot wave. It was the largest wave (the height of a six-story building!) ever surfed by a woman.

⭐ Once, in Portugal, a wave overtook Maya, ripping her life jacket, breaking her leg, and almost drowning her. She recovered and went right back to surfing.

⭐ Her favorite dessert is *brigadeiro*, a Brazilian dish made with condensed milk, chocolate, and butter.

# MC SOFFIA
## rapper

Born February 22, 2004
Brazil

MC Soffia uses her voice and rap lyrics to celebrate Black girls, empower women, and spotlight the history of Black communities in Brazil.

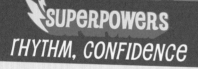

**SUPERPOWERS**
## RHYTHM, CONFIDENCE

★ MC Soffia fell in love with rap at a kids' party. She participated in a workshop where she learned about the elements of hip-hop.

★ MC Soffia was often teased in school for the color of her skin. To help her gain confidence, her mother took her to hip-hop concerts.

★ At 12 years old, she gained international recognition when she performed at the opening ceremony of the 2016 Olympics in Brazil.

★ Her music and lyrics have been taught in schools and included in textbooks to showcase Afro-Brazilian history.

# MEGAN RAPINOE
## SOCCER PLAYER
### Born July 5, 1985
### United States

Together with her team members, Megan Rapinoe fought for female soccer players to be paid the same as men—and they won!

- Megan began playing soccer as a young girl. Her older brother played soccer, too, and her father coached many of the teams that Megan played on.

- Megan was on her high school's honor roll every semester.

- In college, she was badly injured during a game. It could have ended her career. She recovered and never gave up her dream of going professional.

- She likes to dye her hair a shade of purple-pink—a color her hairstylist has called "Rapinko."

**SUPERPOWERS**
**ORIGINALITY, AGILITY**

# MELBA LISTON

## TROMBONIST

January 13, 1926–
April 23, 1999
United States

A talented trombonist, Melba Liston was known for her skills arranging music for prominent jazz musicians.

**SUPERPOWERS**

MUSIC COMPOSITION, STAGE PRESENCE

★ Melba was first inspired to become a trombonist when a traveling music store reached her hometown. Her mother said the trombone was almost bigger than she was, but Melba was determined to play it.

★ Melba's whole family loved music. Her grandfather played the guitar and taught her spirituals and folk songs.

★ At just eight years old, Melba played her own solo show on the local radio! Two years later, she moved to Los Angeles and played alongside musicians in youth bands.

★ She played with musicians like Gerald Wilson and Billie Holiday, and arranged albums for Marvin Gaye, Billy Eckstine and The Supremes.

# MERRITT MOORE
## QUANTUM PHYSICIST & BALLERINA
### Born February 24, 1988
### United States

Merritt Moore combined her love for physics and ballet to create iconic dances with robots.

## SUPERPOWERS
### LOGIC, FINESSE

★ Merritt co-created a film about how physics and ballet work together through movement, light, and wave particles.

★ She decided to get her pilot's license so she could work toward becoming an astronaut. She says, "My dream is to dance on the moon."

★ Merritt and her family listened to audiobooks regularly, made potions, and completed 3-D puzzles. They also had two Great Dane dogs, who chased her and her sister around the house.

★ In college, Merritt would switch between spending time in the lab and the ballet studio. She discovered that dance gave her a new perspective on physics.

# MICHAELA DEPRINCE

## Ballerina

Born January 6, 1995
Sierra Leone and United States

**Michaela DePrince pursued her dream of dance after growing up in Sierra Leone during a period of war.**

⚡SUPERPOWERS *FLEXIBILITY, FOCUS*

 Michaela was orphaned at a young age, and she has a skin condition, called vitiligo, that causes white spots on her neck and chest. Children at the orphanage bullied her for looking different.

 She knew she wanted to learn ballet when she saw a ballerina posing on a magazine cover.

 Michaela was adopted by an American family, along with eight other children. Her adoptive family enrolled her in ballet classes.

 She's performed in dozens of productions and appeared in music videos for pop stars Beyoncé and Madonna.

A picture of a ballerina changed Michaela's life and unlocked her passion. Do pictures ever inspire you or ignite your imagination? Create your own dream board!

Gather glue, a pair of scissors, a piece of paper, and all the magazines in your house (with your grown-up's permission). You can print things from a computer if you don't have magazines.

Find letters and images that show your interests or what you want to achieve. Cut out pictures that show the person you want to become, places you'd like to visit, or anything that brings you joy. Paste them to the paper.

Look back at this collage to remind yourself of your goals, dreams, and hopes for the future.

# MICHELLE KWAN

## FIGURE SKATER

Born July 7, 1980
United States

Michelle Kwan's skill on the ice and pride for her Chinese roots brought visibility to millions of Asian Americans.

**SUPERPOWERS** *energy, grace*

Michelle pursued figure skating alongside her older sister, Karen. Her brother, Ron, pursued a career in ice hockey. The three siblings woke up at 4:30 every morning to skate before school.

When Michelle started competing, she would sleep in her skating costume instead of her pajamas so she wouldn't need to change in the morning.

She's won two Olympic medals, five world championships, and nine US championships.

After retiring from figure skating, she appeared on several TV shows, including *Family Guy*, *Sabrina the Teenage Witch*, and a *Mulan* TV special.

# MIHO NONAKA
## BOULDERER
Born May 21, 1997
Japan

**Miho Nonaka is a special type of mountain climber: a boulderer!**

- Boulderers don't use ropes or harnesses. When Miho climbs rocks and walls, she uses only her strength and flexibility.

- Miho has been climbing since she was nine. She started competing around the world when she was 16.

- She was inspired by her father and her older sister, who both mountain climb. At first, she trained extra hard because she wanted to be a better climber than her sister!

- Miho injured her knee just before the 2021 Olympics but still managed to win the silver medal for Japan.

- She has three cats: Aka, Kona, and Mu.

## SUPERPOWERS
### AMBITION, DEXTERITY

# MIKAILA ULMER

## entrepreneur

Born September 28, 2004
United States

At four years old,
Mikaila Ulmer founded
the company Me & the
Bees Lemonade.

* After getting stung by a bee twice in one week, Mikaila developed a fear of bees. So she did some research. Learning all sorts of cool bee facts helped her overcome her fear of them.

* Mikaila read about how bees make honey, and it gave her a great idea. She had a recipe for lemonade, and she wanted to use a healthy sweetener. Honey was just the thing!

* Mikaila pitched her lemonade business idea to a group of investors on the TV show *Shark Tank*. She came away with $60,000 in funding.

* For every bottle of Me & the Bees lemonade sold, Mikaila donates a portion of the profits to organizations that protect honeybees.

# MILLO CASTRO ZALDARRIAGA

## DRUMMER

Born circa 1922
Cuba

**Despite being told that she was not allowed to be a musician because she was a girl, Millo Castro Zaldarriaga became a world-famous drummer.**

* At first, Millo's father did not approve of his daughter's ambition to be a drummer. But Millo convinced him to find her a music teacher.

* Millo's sister, Cuchito Castro, put together Cuba's first all-girl dance band. Millo joined as a drummer when she was just 10 years old. The band, Anacaona, became popular all over the world.

* When Millo was 15, Anacaona performed at President Franklin D. Roosevelt's birthday party.

* There is a picture book about her called *Drum Dream Girl*.

# MIN JIN LEE
## author

Born November 11, 1968
South Korea
and United States

Min Jin Lee is an award-winning author whose stories explore the Korean immigrant experience.

## ⚡SUPERPOWERS
### FOCUS, IMAGINATION

Min's father used to call her "turtle" because she worked so carefully and slowly.

When she was seven years old, Min and her family immigrated to the United States from South Korea.

Min was a lawyer for several years before deciding to spend all of her time doing what she loved: writing!

Min writes both fiction and nonfiction. In addition to her novels, she has written newspaper and magazine articles.

Her novel *Pachinko* was included on President Obama's recommended reading list.

# MIN MEHTA
## ORTHOPEDIC SURGEON
November 1, 1926–August 23, 2017
Iran, India, and United Kingdom

Min Mehta developed a new way to treat childhood scoliosis—a spine abnormality she suffered from herself.

**SUPERPOWERS** *COMPASSION, INNOVATION*

As a child, Min learned she had a curve in her spine that kept her from sitting or standing straight.

Min had wanted to be a doctor since she was six.

In the 1950s, it was unusual for women to be doctors, and even more unusual for them to be surgeons. When Min first walked through the door of the hospital where she worked, the other doctors were shocked. They had all thought "Min" was a man's name!

Min developed a plaster cast to help young children's spines straighten as they grew. The treatment is now called a Mehta cast.

✦ Miriam had always loved to sing. As a child, she used to sneak into church choir rehearsals.

✦ Miriam began performing in the United States in 1959. She introduced many new people to South African music.

✦ Many of her songs protested apartheid—the cruel laws that discriminated against Black and multiracial people in South Africa. To punish Miriam, the South African government would not let her back into the country. She was not able to return for 31 years.

✦ Miriam became known as a symbol of protest against apartheid. She was called Mother Africa.

# MIRIAM MAKEBA
## SINGER & ACTIVIST
March 4, 1932–
November 9, 2008
South Africa, United
States, and Guinea

Miriam Makeba used her music to challenge the unfair laws of her home country.

# MISTY COPELAND

## BALLERINA

Born September 10, 1982
United States

Misty Copeland was the first Black female principal dancer with the American Ballet Theatre—one of the most well-known ballet companies in the world.

## SUPERPOWERS
### BALANCE, GRACE

- When Misty was 13 years old, she was living with her siblings and her mother in a motel. A visit to a Boys & Girls Club introduced Misty to ballet.

- When Misty first started dancing, she was told she was too old to become a great dancer and that she had the wrong kind of body. Misty kept dancing anyway.

- Misty makes time in her busy schedule to mentor young people. In 2014, she was appointed to the President's Council on Sports, Fitness & Nutrition.

- She has written a memoir and two children's books.

# MURIEL TRAMIS

## VIDEO GAME DESIGNER

Born September 16, 1958
Martinique and France

**Muriel Tramis took her love of games and turned it digital, helping to design some of the earliest computer video games. She is known as the first Black woman video game designer.**

 **SUPERPOWER** *creativity*

 Muriel loved playing games as a kid—crossword puzzles, board games, word games, any kind of game! She even invented games of her own.

 In the early 1980s, computers were first starting to be used for gaming, and the first computer video games were being released. Muriel then started working as a video game designer.

 Muriel used her video games to teach others about Black history in Martinique. She once said she had a "responsibility to speak for her ancestors."

✳ She used many elements of her home country in her games. One game featured a recipe for a Caribbean vegetable dish called callaloo.

Have you ever had an idea for a game?
What is it about? Where is it set?
Does it incorporate your experiences
or your culture, like Muriel's games
do? What are the rules? How do
players interact? Grab a pen and
paper and start brainstorming!

# MUZOON ALMELLEHAN

## EDUCATION ACTIVIST

Born circa April 1998
Syria and United Kingdom

Muzoon Almellehan began
working as an activist for
girls' education before
she was a teenager.

**SUPERPOWER** *persistence*

When she was 11, Muzoon
and her family had to flee
Syria. She was allowed to
pack just one bag. She filled
it with her schoolbooks,
saying, "These books are
my future."

For several years, Muzoon
and her family lived in a
refugee camp. Although the
camp had schools, Muzoon
discovered many girls did
not attend. She visited
parents in the camp and
encouraged them to send
their daughters to school.

Muzoon became a Goodwill
Ambassador for UNICEF in
2017. At the time, she was
the youngest person ever to
be chosen for the role.

She has been on the BBC's
list of 100 inspirational
women and *Time*
magazine's list of most
influential teens. She was
one of *Glamour*'s Women of
the Year in 2017.

# MYA-ROSE CRAIG
## ORNITHOLOGIST & ACTIVIST
### Born May 7, 2002
### United Kingdom

With a passion for conservation, Mya-Rose Craig is a birdwatcher, blogger, and environmentalist.

+ Mya-Rose started a blog called *Birdgirl* when she was 11.

+ At the age of 17, she spotted a harpy eagle in the Amazon rain forest in Brazil. With the sighting, she became the youngest person to have seen half the birds in the world. That's 5,000 species!

+ Mya-Rose was distressed to learn that some famous conservationists in history had been cruel to the Indigenous populations that lived on the land they were fighting to preserve. She decided to combine her conservation activism with support for Indigenous people.

+ She works with Black and brown teenagers, encouraging them to explore the field of environmental science by hosting nature camps and posting on social media.

# NADINE BURKE HARRIS
## PEDIATRICIAN
Born October 9, 1975
Canada, Jamaica, and United States

Nadine Burke Harris focuses her work on the links between trauma and physical health. She wants to take care of children's brains as well as their bodies.

**SUPERPOWER** *empathy*

* Science and medicine run in Nadine's family. Her father was a chemist, and her mother was a nurse. Both contributed to her love of learning.

* Nadine knew that stress and anxiety can contribute to sickness, so she created an organization to research treating stress in children and young people.

* She was California's first-ever surgeon general! She was also the first Black person and the first woman to have the position of surgeon general in the country.

* Mindfulness is an important part of her treatment programs.

* She loves gardening and grows her own fruits and vegetables.

# NANCY WAKE

## SPY

August 30, 1912–
August 7, 2011
New Zealand and France

Nancy Wake was a resistance fighter and spy during World War II. Her work kept many, many soldiers alive.

**SUPERPOWER** STEALTH

+ In the 1930s, Nancy was on a trip to Vienna when she saw Nazis attacking Jewish citizens. She promised she would find a way to help stop them.

+ As a young woman living in France, Nancy went to parties and met a lot of people. She used her social connections to help refugees leave the country.

+ Nancy trained with the British Special Operations Executive. She parachuted back into France with other resistance fighters to hide weapons and prepare for Allied armies to arrive.

+ The German army nicknamed Nancy "the White Mouse" because she was so difficult to catch.

+ Even though her work was dangerous, Nancy claimed she was too busy to be afraid.

# NANDI BUSHELL

## Drummer

Born April 28, 2010
South Africa and
United Kingdom

**Nandi Bushell's love for drumming set social media on fire! Her talent caught the attention of her many fans as well as famous musicians.**

## ⚡SUPERPOWERS
### ENERGY, BEATS

⭐ One of Nandi's earliest musical influences was the British rock band the Beatles. She especially loved Ringo Starr, the drummer.

⭐ In 2020, she challenged Dave Grohl, a famous musician, to an online drum-off. To her surprise, the musician responded with his own video!

⭐ Nandi got to live out a dream in 2021: She played with Dave Grohl and his band the Foo Fighters onstage at a concert.

⭐ The musician Lenny Kravitz gave Nandi a custom drum set as a gift.

⭐ She also plays guitar, keyboard, and saxophone.

# NANNY OF THE MAROONS

## QUEEN

Circa 1686–1733
Jamaica

Along with other enslaved Africans, Nanny of the Maroons escaped bondage in Jamaica and moved to a remote part of the country. There, she set up a new community and became known as Queen Nanny.

**SUPERPOWER**

*resilience*

* Nanny set up a Maroon community—a secret, hidden community made of escapees—where she became the leader. The community became known as Nanny Town.

* Nanny was a strong military leader who trained her people in camouflage, defense, and guerilla warfare.

* She passed down legends, music, and customs from Africa. Nanny encouraged her people to remember and continue their heritage.

* There is a statue of Queen Nanny near the site of Nanny Town, and her picture is on Jamaica's $500 bill.

# NAOMI OSAKA

## TENNIS PLAYER

Born October 16, 1997
Japan and United States

**Naomi Osaka is a tennis pro, a four-time Grand Slam champion, and the first Asian player to be ranked #1 in the world.**

**SUPERPOWERS** *CONSISTENCY, FOCUS*

 Naomi is half Haitian and half Japanese. She represents Japan while playing. At first, Japanese fans were surprised to see that she had brown skin.

 Naomi and her family used to watch Serena and Venus Williams on television. Naomi's father coached Naomi and her sister, just like Serena and Venus's father coached them. In 2018, Naomi played against Serena, her longtime hero. Naomi shocked the crowd by winning!

 Naomi can serve a tennis ball at more than 120 miles an hour. That's faster than a cheetah and faster than most roller coasters.

 Another one of her interests is fashion. She has designed swimwear and athletic clothing.

**YOUR TURN!**

While playing in the US Open during the COVID-19 pandemic, Naomi wore a different mask every game. Each mask bore the name of someone who had suffered violence because of their race.

What do you care about? The environment? Endangered species? Civil rights? Access to education? Design a shirt or a mask that gets people thinking about your cause.

# NEFERTITI
## QUEEN
### Circa 1370 BCE– circa 1330 BCE
### Egypt

As queen of Egypt, Nefertiti took on many roles usually reserved for men. She was a powerful and puzzling queen—both her birth and her death remain a mystery.

## SUPERPOWER *LEADERSHIP*

* The name *Nefertiti* means "a beautiful woman has come," but no one is completely sure where she came from. Some historians believe Nefertiti was a princess from Syria, and others believe she was born in Egypt.

* Paintings and drawings of Nefertiti show her leading religious ceremonies, driving chariots, and fighting in battles.

* Her reign ended when she disappeared! There is no record of her death, and no evidence she was buried in her family's tomb.

* In 2015, archaeologists discovered a secret room in the tomb of Pharaoh Tutankhamen (often called King Tut). They wondered if Nefertiti's mummy might be inside. Unfortunately, there's no way (yet!) to open the room without damaging the artifacts in the tomb.

# NELLIE BLY

## reporter

May 5, 1864–
January 27, 1922
United States

Nellie Bly's investigative reporting took her around the world in record time.

**SUPERPOWERS**

*CURIOSITY, BOLDNESS*

* When Nellie was 18, she read an article that said women should stay home and not have jobs. She wrote a letter to the newspaper that impressed the editor so much he offered her a job.

* In order to expose the terrible way patients were treated at a mental institution, Nellie checked in as a patient. She experienced the horrifying conditions for herself and wrote about what she saw.

* In 1873, a popular book called *Around the World in 80 Days* was published. To test if the trip could really be done, Nellie packed a bag and traveled by ship, donkey, rickshaw, and horse. She made the journey in 72 days, 6 hours, 11 minutes, and 14 seconds.

* "Nellie Bly" was a pen name. Nellie and her newspaper editor chose the name from a song.

# NEMONTE NENQUIMO
## CLIMATE ACTIVIST
### Born 1986
### Ecuador

Nemonte Nenquimo fought to save the Amazon rain forest and land of the Waorani people from oil companies.

The Waorani tribe has lived in and protected the forests of Ecuador for generations. When Nemonte learned companies were cutting down trees and poisoning the water with chemicals, she circulated petitions and helped make maps of the Waorani's land.

Nemonte found out that Ecuador's government planned to sell parts of the Amazon rain forest to oil companies. She filed a lawsuit against the government and won her case.

Because of Nemonte, 500,000 acres of land were saved.

In 2020, *Time* magazine named her one of the most influential people in the world.

**SUPERPOWER** *courage*

Her name translates to "many stars, face of the sun."

# NIKI YANG
## animator & voice actor
Born September 19, 1982
South Korea
and United States

**SUPERPOWERS**
artistry, humor

Niki Yang has drawn cartoons and performed the voices of animated characters for shows like *Adventure Time*.

Niki's family expected her to get married and take care of a household. But she had other plans—she wanted to make comic books! She'd never heard of a school for drawing comics, so she decided to get a degree in animation.

In college, Niki discovered she loved storyboarding. A storyboard is a set of drawings that tell the story of a film. Directors and animators use storyboards to figure out what each scene will look like.

Niki is the voice of several cartoon characters, including one who speaks Korean.

She loves getting mail from Korean American fans who are thrilled to hear their family's language on television.

# NINA SIMONE

## SINGER

February 21, 1933–
April 21, 2003
United States

A gifted jazz singer, Nina Simone infused her songs with emotion. Some of her songs became stirring anthems for the US civil rights movement.

- Nina started training as a classical pianist when she was five years old.

- At Nina's first performance at age 12, her parents were told to leave the front row to make room for white audience members. Nina refused to play until her parents were given back their seats.

- During her career, Nina recorded more than 40 albums.

- She was good friends with playwright Lorraine Hansberry. One of Nina's most well-known songs, "To Be Young, Gifted, and Black," was written in memory of Lorraine. The words were taken from the title of the play Lorraine had been working on before she died.

**SUPERPOWER**
MOVING VOCALS

# NOOR INAYAT KHAN

## SPY

January 1, 1914–
September 13, 1944
Russia, United Kingdom,
and France

Sent to France to spy for England during World War II, Noor Inayat Khan was the first female radio operator.

## SUPERPOWERS
### BRAVERY, STEALTH

✦ Noor's father was a Muslim prince from India.

✦ Noor wrote children's stories. Many of them were published in French magazines and heard on the radio.

✦ At the beginning of World War II, Noor joined the Women's Auxiliary Air Force in England. Eventually, she was recruited to join a group of radio operators who sent secret messages between the British and the French.

✦ Noor's code name as a radio operator was Madeleine.

✦ Sometimes spies were caught and arrested. When this happened to members of Noor's team, she would take over their work. At one point, she was doing the work of six spies on her own.

# NOURA SAKKIJHA

## entrepreneur

Born August 30, 1985
Jordan and Canada

Noura used her knowledge of industrial engineering and the jewelry industry to create a company that sells handcrafted jewelry.

## SUPERPOWERS
### CREATIVITY, PROBLEM-SOLVING

Noura was tired of seeing ads telling women that jewelry should be given to them as gifts. She thought women should be comfortable buying jewelry for themselves and wearing it whenever they want.

She made jewelry more affordable by selling it directly to the customer, rather than selling it to stores that would sell it to consumers.

Noura works ethically. All her diamonds are sourced from socially responsible dealers.

To relax, she loves to watch TV and do yoga.

# NZINGA OF NDONGO AND MATAMBA

## QUEEN

Circa 1583–
December 17, 1663
Angola

Nzinga was a fearless queen remembered for her skill at negotiation. She fought for decades to keep her kingdoms independent.

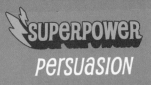
- When the African kingdom of Ndongo was under attack from Portugal, Nzinga convinced the Portuguese governor to agree to a treaty.

- Nzinga took over the throne when her brother died and continued to fight. Although she was a clever military strategist, she was eventually defeated.

- Losing her throne did not stop Nzinga. She became ruler of the kingdom of Matamba and continued her fight from there.

- In Matamba, Nzinga built up her army by giving sanctuary to people who had escaped enslavement.

- After 30 years of battling Portugal, Nzinga reclaimed part of Ndongo and became queen of both Ndongo and Matamba.

# OCTAVIA E. BUTLER

## AUTHOR

June 22, 1947–
February 24, 2006
United States

Science fiction writer
Octavia E. Butler
created new worlds,
alien landscapes, and
futuristic societies
with her words.

✦ Octavia was 6 feet tall by the time she was 15.

✦ Because she was dyslexic, she had to take her time reading and writing, and she struggled with spelling. Despite that, she went on to study creative writing.

✦ During her lifetime, most science fiction writers were white men. Most publishers didn't think Octavia's books would sell. But once she found a publisher, many of her novels became best sellers.

✦ Octavia was the first science fiction writer to win a MacArthur Fellowship—a prestigious grant for people with "exceptional creativity."

# OLGA KORBUT

## GYMNAST

Born May 16, 1955
Belarus
and United States

Olga Korbut was 17 years old when she won three gold medals and one silver medal at the 1972 Olympics.

+ Olga worked with her coach to create new gymnastic moves that no one had ever seen before.

+ When gymnastic judges didn't approve of the way Olga was trying new things, she said, "Let me—I will show the world what gymnastics looks like."

## SUPERPOWERS
### AGILITY, FLEXIBILITY

+ She was the first gymnast to perform a backward release on the uneven bars. The trick is now known as the Korbut flip.

+ Olga was also the first gymnast to do a backward somersault on the balance beam.

+ She received so many letters from fans that her hometown had to hire a postal worker just for her!

# OPRAH WINFREY

## TV HOST, ACTOR, & BUSINESSWOMAN

Born January 29, 1954
United States

Oprah Winfrey's ability to connect with people made her one of the most well-known television personalities of all time.

**SUPERPOWERS**
CONNECTION, GENEROSITY

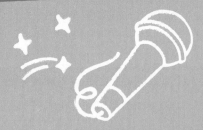

⭐ Oprah's father was very strict. He made her write a book report every week.

⭐ Oprah was fired from her first news anchor job on television. She then took over a small talk show in Chicago. It became enormously popular and was renamed *The Oprah Winfrey Show*.

⭐ A lot of her charity work has focused on education for girls. She's opened a school for girls in South Africa.

⭐ Her favorite book is *To Kill a Mockingbird*.

⭐ She doesn't like it when people chew or smack gum.

# PAT SUMMITT

## BASKETBALL COACH

June 14, 1952–June 28, 2016
United States

Pat Summitt was a basketball coach whose record of 1,098 wins in 38 seasons helped make women's basketball the sport it is today.

⭐ Pat grew up on a farm. During the day, she baled hay, and in the evening, she played basketball in the loft of the barn.

⭐ In third grade, she was playing on the eighth grade basketball team.

⭐ Just before the 1976 Olympics, Pat injured her knee. The doctor was afraid she wouldn't be able to play again, but she did—and she helped lead her team to a silver medal.

⭐ She became the coach of a women's basketball team at just 22 years old. At the time, women's sports weren't taken seriously, and the team didn't have much support. Pat held a donut sale to pay for team uniforms.

## SUPERPOWERS

ENERGY, COMMUNICATION

# PATRICIA BATH

## OPHTHALMOLOGIST & INVENTOR

November 4, 1942–May 30, 2019
United States

When Patricia Bath started medical school, she was determined to make healthy eyesight a basic right for all. Her groundbreaking work has helped treat eye disease in countless people.

**SUPERPOWER**
*INNOVATION*

- Patricia's mother bought her her first chemistry set.

- Patricia discovered that Black people were twice as likely as white people to have problems with their vision. She organized and trained volunteers to teach people in Black communities about eye care and help them find eye clinics.

- Patricia is best known for her invention of the Laserphaco Probe, which made eye surgery easier and less painful for patients. The invention restored the sight of some people who had been blind for many years.

- With the Laserphaco Probe, Patricia became the first Black woman to patent a medical device.

# PAULINE LÉON

## revolutionary

September 28, 1768–
October 5, 1838
France

Pauline Léon believed that women were as essential to the French Revolution as men. She encouraged other women to get involved.

- Pauline was the daughter of a chocolatier in Paris. After her father died, she helped take care of her five younger siblings as well as run the family chocolate business.

- She was part of the class of people in France called the third estate at the time. The term referred to people who did not own land and were not priests.

- Pauline was one of the founders of the Society of Revolutionary Republican Women, a group that met to discuss ways to sabotage enemies of the Revolution.

- She demanded that women be allowed to carry weapons. She also tried hard to get permission to form a female militia.

# PEGGY GUGGENHEIM
## art collector
August 26, 1898–December 23, 1979
United States and Italy

Peggy Guggenheim collected paintings by artists experimenting with new and exciting styles. Her collection would become one of the most important and valuable in the world.

+ Peggy lost her father when she was 14 years old. He was a passenger aboard the *Titanic* when it sank in the Atlantic Ocean.

+ Peggy loved abstract, cubist, and surrealist art. Because gallery owners and museums did not yet appreciate these styles, she was able to buy paintings for far less money than they would eventually be worth.

+ To keep her paintings from being destroyed by bombs during World War II, Peggy hid them in a friend's barn.

+ She liked to shock people. As a teenager, she once shaved off her eyebrows.

**SUPERPOWERS**
INDEPENDENCE, VISION

# PHIONA MUTESI
## CHESS PLAYER
### Born 1996
### Uganda

Phiona Mutesi discovered a game that changed her life. She became the first woman in Uganda to earn a chess title.

## SUPERPOWERS
### FORWARD THINKING, STRATEGY

Phiona had to leave school at age six to help her mother sell maize, fetch water, and keep up the household.

One day, she saw her brother through the window of a sports club playing chess. When the coach noticed her, he invited her inside.

Phiona discovered she had a natural gift for the game. She was soon winning against her coach!

Her dream is to become a chess grandmaster, which is the highest title a chess player can have.

In 2016, Disney made a movie about Phiona's life called *Queen of Katwe*.

# POLICARPA SALAVARRIETA

## SPY

### Circa 1795–November 14, 1817
### Colombia

**Policarpa Salavarrieta was a revolutionary who wanted her country to be independent from Spanish rule.**

 **SUPERPOWER** *DEFIANCE*

* No one knows what Policarpa's real name actually was—she kept it secret. Everyone knew her as Policarpa or La Pola.

* Policarpa was a skilled seamstress, and she used her sewing skills to spy on families that were loyal to the king of Spain. She listened closely while working on ladies' dresses and passed on what she learned to revolutionaries.

* She was eventually captured, but she refused to give up any information, including the names of her allies and friends.

* There is a statue of Policarpa in Bogotá, Colombia. Her face is also on the 10,000 pesos bill. Colombia's Day of the Woman takes place on the date of her death.

YOUR TURN!

Need to send a secret message? Use a secret code! One easy code is called Every Second Letter. To read a code written this way, read every second letter. Then go back to the beginning and read every letter you skipped.

Deccode this message:
E C A A D N T Y H O I U S R

Step 1:
E C A A D N T Y H O I U S R

Step 2:
E C A A D N T Y H O I U S R

Flip this book upside—down to see the answer. Then try writing your own secret message using the Every Second Letter Code!

* Poly was made fun of as a child for being biracial. She dropped out of school when she was 15 and ran away from home.

* Poly called herself "an ordinary tough kid from an ordinary tough street."

* She chose the stage name Poly Styrene after the material polystyrene, which is plastic and disposable. It was her way of poking fun at pop stardom.

* Many punk rock bands and artists say they were influenced by her work, including Bikini Kill and Neneh Cherry.

# POLY STYRENE
## PUNK ROCKER
### July 3, 1957–April 25, 2011
### United Kingdom

Poly Styrene was the stage name of Marianne Joan Elliot-Said, who sung for the punk band X-Ray Spex.

# POORNA MALAVATH

## MOUNTAINEER

Born June 10, 2000
India

**At age 13, Poorna Malavath became the youngest girl to reach the top of Mount Everest.**

* Poorna said a school she attended made her feel "like a newborn butterfly emerging from her cocoon." It was there she had her first mountain-climbing workshop.

* It took Poorna and her team 52 days to reach the top of Mount Everest.

* During her journey, Poorna saw the bodies of climbers who had not survived. She said the sight made her legs shiver.

* Because the cold made it hard to eat, she and her team mainly relied on chocolates, dried fruits, and liquids to survive their climb.

**SUPERPOWER** *endurance*

# PURNIMA DEVI BARMAN

## WILDLIFE BIOLOGIST

Birthdate unknown
India

Purnima Devi Barman
works to educate
people about a species
of stork and save it
from extinction.

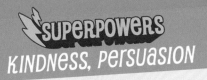

## SUPERPOWERS
### KINDNESS, PERSUASION

+ The hargila is a large stork that could once be found all over Southeast Asia. Now it lives in one small part of India. Most people thought the birds were smelly and gross, because they often look for food in garbage dumps and they eat dead animals. But Purnima knows they are special.

+ Purnima loves that the hargilas have bright, sky-blue eyes.

+ She pulled together a group of women she calls the "Hargila Army." The women sometimes wear elaborate headdresses that look like the head and shoulders of the hargila stork and perform songs and dances.

+ Purnima says Jane Goodall is a wonderful role model for everyone— herself included!

# QIU JIN

## revolutionary

November 8, 1875–July 15, 1907
China

Qiu Jin was not content with the role of women in 19th-century China. She became a poet, a revolutionary, and a champion of women's rights.

**SUPERPOWERS** *verse, swordsmanship*

Qiu Jin was interested in politics, dressed in men's clothes, and knew how to use a sword.

Many Chinese revolutionaries were working and studying in Japan. Qiu Jin became a leader in the Chinese community there.

She started a magazine called *Chinese Women's Journal* and opened a school. It appeared to be a school to train sports teachers, but Qiu Jin was really training revolutionaries.

Her secret work was discovered, and she was arrested. She refused to confess or give her captors any information. Instead, she recited poetry.

# RACHEL CARSON

## Marine BIOLOGIST & AUTHOR

May 27, 1907–
April 14, 1964
United States

Rachel Carson was a scientist whose writing helped begin the global environmental movement.

- Rachel's mother taught her to see the beauty in the natural world around her.

- Rachel loved to write about her explorations of the forests, streams, and fields near her home.

- Her articles and books about the ocean introduced many people to the wonders of sea life.

- Rachel was one of the first environmental scientists to speak out about the dangers of pesticides. She wrote a book describing the impact chemicals had on wildlife.

- Chemical companies were outraged by Rachel's work, but other scientists supported her. Her work led to a ban on the pesticide DDT.

- Growing up, she loved to read Beatrix Potter's books.

# RENATA FLORES

## SINGER-SONGWRITER

Born March 20, 2001
Peru

Renata Flores recorded a version of Michael Jackson's song "The Way You Make Me Feel" with the lyrics in Quechua, a language spoken by the Indigenous people of Peru. Her video went viral.

**SUPERPOWERS**

*MUSICALITY, UNIQUE STYLE*

+ Renata was exposed to instruments growing up because her parents owned a music school.

+ She composes songs about Indigenous rights and the social conflicts in Peru.

+ Renata writes her songs in Spanish, and her grandmothers help her translate them into Quechua.

+ She can often be seen rocking long braids and bold earrings.

# REYNA DUONG
## CHEF
Born May 30, 1977
Vietnam and
United States

Reyna Duong is the chef and owner of a Vietnamese sandwich shop and a fierce voice for equity and safety in the workplace.

Reyna hated cooking as a kid. She preferred to be outside climbing trees.

When she first opened her Vietnamese sandwich shop, Reyna was told that her food might be too foreign for the customers of Dallas, Texas. She refused to change any of her recipes—and the customers kept coming.

Reyna welcomes neurodivergent workers, including her brother Sang, into her kitchen. Sang has trouble reading, so Reyna uses a color-coding system for drink orders.

She can eat 10 pounds of crawfish in one sitting!

# RIHANNA
## entrepreneur & singer
Born February 20, 1988
Barbados and United States

Rihanna is an international music sensation and entrepreneur whose beauty brand is changing the face of makeup companies.

Music helped Rihanna cope with her parents' divorce. As a teenager, she formed a band with two of her classmates.

Rihanna lived in Barbados. When a music producer came for vacation, a friend of Rihanna's convinced him to give the band an audition. The producer asked Rihanna to come to the US to record a solo album instead.

Rihanna's third album made her a household name. She was nominated for several Grammy Awards, winning the award for best rap/sung collaboration.

**SUPERPOWERS**
**AMBITION, STYLE**

Rihanna is also an actor and producer. She's worked on films, television series, and commercials.

When her company Fenty Beauty launched, it included 40 shades of foundation. Other makeup brands soon began introducing colors to match more skin tones too. Reporters called this "the Fenty Effect."

# ROSA PARKS

## CIVIL rIGHTS aCTIVIST

February 4, 1913–
October 24, 2005
United States

Rosa Parks refused to give
up her seat on a city bus to
make more room for white
passengers to sit down. Her
actions ignited a movement.

When a bus driver asked
Rosa to give up her seat
for a white passenger,
Rosa said no. She was
arrested. Black people in
Montgomery, Alabama,
rallied behind her and
started a bus boycott
that lasted 381 days.

The civil rights leader
E. D. Nixon took Rosa's
case all the way to the
Supreme Court. As a
result, segregation on
buses was declared
unconstitutional.

In 1999, she was awarded
the Congressional Gold
Medal.

On the 50th anniversary
of Rosa's arrest, cities
across the country left
empty seats on buses in
her honor.

**SUPERPOWER** *CONVICTION*

# ROSALIE ABELLA

## JUDGE

Born July 1, 1946
Germany and Canada

Rosalie Abella became a judge after just four years of being a lawyer. Her career was a series of historical firsts.

## ⚡SUPERPOWERS OPTIMISM, COMMUNICATION

- In Canada, Rosalie was the first Jewish woman to become a judge, the first Jewish woman to be a member of the Supreme Court, one of the youngest judges in the country's history, and the first person to become a judge while pregnant!

- When she stepped down from serving on the Supreme Court, she was its longest-serving member.

- When asked about her work, Rosalie said, "I had no mission on the Supreme Court except to really be a good judge."

- Rosalie has a degree in classical piano from the Royal Conservatory of Music.

# ROSALIND FRANKLIN

## CHEMIST & X-RAY CRYSTALLOGRAPHER

July 25, 1920–
April 16, 1958
United Kingdom

During her scientific career, Rosalind Franklin studied coal and viruses at the microscopic level. Her most important work was discovering new information about DNA.

⭐ Rosalind was an excellent student, except in one class: music! Her teacher said she sang "almost in tune."

⭐ When Rosalind became a scientist, no one knew what DNA looked like. She spent countless hours trying to take photographs of DNA with X-rays and figured out how to make her machines take more accurate pictures.

⭐ She and her team finally took an amazing picture, which they named *Photograph 51*. The picture provided key information about what DNA fibers actually look like.

⭐ Another team of scientists used Rosalind's photograph and research to finish their own work. They won a Nobel Prize for discovering the structure of DNA. It took many years before Rosalind got credit for her incredible contributions to science.

# ROSELI OCAMPO-FRIEDMANN

## MICROBIOLOGIST

November 23, 1937–
September 4, 2005
The Philippines and
United States

**Roseli Ocampo-Friedmann traveled the world with her husband studying algae and microorganisms no one had known existed before.**

SUPERPOWER
**aDVENTUROUS SPIRIT**

⭐ Most scientists thought there was no life on the cold, dry mountains of Antarctica's Ross Valley. Roseli and her husband discovered microorganisms living there, and Roseli was able to bring some back to her laboratory to study them.

⭐ People who are good with plants are sometimes said to have a "green thumb." The joke was that Roseli had a "blue-green thumb," because of her work with algae.

⭐ She spent her life traveling to extreme environments and collecting specimens. She found more than 1,000 types of microorganisms.

⭐ Some scientists believe that Roseli and her husband's work can help shed light on the kinds of life that exist on other planets in the solar system.

# ROSETTA THARPE

## GUITARIST

March 20, 1915–
October 9, 1973
United States

**Rosetta Tharpe was a gospel superstar and the Godmother of Rock and Roll.**

✳ By the time she was six, Rosetta was playing her guitar in churches all over the South, performing gospel music with her mother.

✳ She eventually started playing her music in nightclubs under the name Sister Rosetta Tharpe.

✳ Due to segregation at the time, Rosetta had to stay in different hotels and eat in different restaurants than her white bandmates.

✳ Many renowned rock stars were influenced by Rosetta's music and skill with the guitar, including Elvis Presley and Chuck Berry.

✳ In 2018, Rosetta was voted into the Rock & Roll Hall of Fame.

# ROXANNE SHANTÉ
## rapper

Born November 9, 1969
United States

---

* Roxanne won her first rap battle when she was 10 years old.

* Male rappers didn't like that Roxanne won so many rap battles. Once, a judge scored her low on purpose to keep her from winning.

* At 14, Roxanne released her first single, "Roxanne's Revenge," which sold more than 250,000 copies. The song was about a woman fighting back against men harassing her.

* "Roxanne's Revenge" was recorded in just 10 minutes, because Roxanne was in a rush. She needed to get home to help her mom with the laundry!

* In 2017, a film about her life, *Roxanne Roxanne,* was released.

**Roxanne Shanté is known as the first female battle rapper. She paved the way for other women in the field.**

SUPERPOWERS
AUDACITY, RHYME

# RUBY BRIDGES
## CIVIL RIGHTS ACTIVIST
Born September 8, 1954
United States

Ruby Bridges became a symbol of civil rights in the United States when she was the first Black student to desegregate the all-white William Frantz Elementary School.

### ⚡SUPERPOWERS
### BRAVERY, OPTIMISM

✦ More than 500 students were taken out of the school by their parents, all because they didn't want Ruby, a Black student, going there.

✦ Many of the teachers at Ruby's school quit. They didn't want to teach a Black student. Barbara Henry left her job in Boston to come to New Orleans to teach Ruby.

✦ For a year, Ruby received her education in an empty classroom.

✦ After she graduated high school, Ruby worked as a travel agent for 15 years.

# RUTH BADER GINSBURG

## SUPREME COURT JUSTICE

March 15, 1933–
September 18, 2020
United States

Ruth Bader Ginsburg made history as the second woman—and first Jewish woman—to serve on the US Supreme Court. She believed in women's rights and social justice.

- When Ruth went to Harvard for law school, she was one of only eight women in a class of 500.

- She was married to her husband Martin for 56 years. She said he was "the only young man I dated who cared that I had a brain."

- Her lace collars were her way of showing that she was unapologetic for being a woman.

- One of Ruth's collars was a rainbow-striped beaded necklace from Ecuador, showing her support for the LGBTQIA+ community.

- She kept to a strict workout routine—even into her 80s.

## SUPERPOWERS

INTELLIGENCE, DETERMINATION

# RUTH E. CARTER
## COSTUME DESIGNER
### Born April 10, 1960
### United States

**Ruth E. Carter is an Academy Award–winning costume designer who has created looks for dozens of films and TV shows.**

**⚡SUPERPOWER** *creativity*

 Ruth was the first Black costume designer to win an Academy Award, which she received for her work on the movie *Black Panther*.

 Ruth has worked on seven films with comedian and actor Eddie Murphy, including *Dr. Doolittle 2* and *Coming 2 America*. Eddie says Ruth is "on the Mount Rushmore of costume designers."

 As a young person, she fell in love with storytelling. She said, "I recited poetry to anybody who would listen!"

 While working on *Black Panther*, Ruth studied patterns and styles from different African tribes. She used the colors of African liberation: red, black, and green.

The superheroes in *Black Panther* wear sleek costumes they can move and fight in, with patterns, colors, and elements that represent African culture and history. What would your superhero costume look like? Would you have a cape? Tall boots? A utility belt? Consider colors, patterns, and elements that represent you. Then design your costume.

# SAMANTHA CRISTOFORETTI

## astronaut

Born April 26, 1977
Italy

Samantha Cristoforetti was the third European woman to travel to space. Her adventures have taken her from the bottom of the sea to the International Space Station.

## SUPERPOWER *DEDICATION*

Samantha was a fighter pilot in the Italian Air Force.

When she applied to join the European Space Agency's space program, there were more than 8,000 applicants. Six were chosen. One of them was Samantha!

Samantha trained for space at the bottom of a deep pool. She swam in her spacesuit, practiced putting equipment together underwater, and even learned to fight underwater.

She studied both Russian and Chinese while training to be an astronaut.

One of her favorite snacks is dried apples.

# SAMARRIA BREVARD

## SKATEBOARDER

Born September 22, 1993
United States

Samarria Brevard is a professional skateboarder and the first Black woman to win a medal in the X Games.

+ Even though she learned to skateboard in skate parks, Samarria prefers street skateboarding because she finds it more challenging.

+ Before she was a skateboarder, Samarria was a basketball player. She says the two sports are similar, because they depend on flexibility and footwork.

+ Samarria was the first Black woman to win the Kimberley Diamond Cup Skateboarding World Championship.

+ Her brother is her favorite skater.

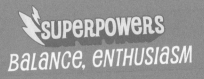
SUPERPOWERS
BALANCE, ENTHUSIASM

# SANDRA AGUEBOR-EKPERUOH

## MECHANIC
### Born 1972
### Nigeria

The first female mechanic in Nigeria, Sandra Aguebor-Ekperuoh fixes cars and teaches other women across the country how to do it too.

SUPERPOWER *SELF-SUFFICIENCY*

+ When Sandra was 13, she had a dream that made her decide her destiny was to fix cars.

+ Sandra created the Lady Mechanic Initiative to train other women to be auto mechanics. She wanted to make sure they were never stranded in unsafe areas.

+ She's trained more than 2,000 women who are employed in garages across her country.

+ Many men in her life have told her that women can't be mechanics. Her father was not one of them. He let her work in his auto shop.

+ Her story was made into a musical, *Lady Mechanics*.

# SANDRA DAY O'CONNOR

## SUPREME COURT JUSTICE

Born March 26, 1930
United States

Sandra Day O'Conner was an attorney and politician. She was the first female justice to serve on the US Supreme Court.

## SUPERPOWERS
### BRAINS, FAIRNESS

Sandra spent her early years on her family's ranch in Arizona. The closest neighbors were 25 miles away!

Sandra was a star student. She skipped two grades and enrolled in college at Stanford University when she was 16 years old.

After graduating law school at the top of her class, Sandra called more than 40 firms looking for a job, but no one would hire a female lawyer. Finally, she found a job working for free.

Over time, she became concerned that kids didn't know much about civics. After she retired from the court, she created a website to help kids learns about democracy.

# SARAH FULLER

## soccer player & football player

Born June 20, 1999
United States

Sarah Fuller is a soccer goalie who also played college football. She was the first player to sign up with the Minnesota Aurora, a women's professional soccer team.

* Even when she was in high school, Sarah could kick a ball 60 yards. That's the length of more than two Olympic swimming pools!

* The summer before college, Sarah broke her foot and had to sit on the bench. But that didn't stop her from cheering on her teammates.

* She joined her college football team, becoming the first woman to kick for a Power Five game—the highest level of college football in the US.

* For her groundbreaking kick, Sarah wore lucky socks and a helmet that said "Play Like a Girl."

## SUPERPOWERS
### POWERFUL KICKS, SPORTSMANSHIP

# SARINYA SRISAKUL

## Firefighter

Born circa 1980
United States

Sarinya Srisakul was the first Asian female firefighter to join the New York City Fire Department.

* The only woman trainee who went through a tough three-month boot camp, Sarinya learned survival skills, like how to fight fires and move and position huge ladders.

* Her family is from Thailand. She speaks several languages, which helps her serve New York's diverse population.

* Sarinya defines "heroism" as helping other people.

* She graduated from art school before working with low-income New Yorkers with HIV/AIDS. She said she "found her calling" as a firefighter after the September 11 attacks.

## SUPERPOWERS
### Bravery, Compassion

# SASHA HUBER

## ARTIST

Born April 24, 1975
Switzerland and Finland

**Sasha Huber uses mixed media, performance, film, and photography to comment on politics and colonial history.**

**SUPERPOWERS** *HONESTY, INGENUITY*

 Sasha's mother was from Haiti. Sasha grew up in Switzerland with relatives from 10 countries.

 When it was time to go to college, Sasha decided to study graphic design.

 Much of her work investigates the effects of colonialism, which is when a country takes over and exploits the people of another country.

 She once used a staple gun to make portraits of Christopher Columbus and the British rulers who took over Haiti.

 Her favorite city to visit is Rio de Janeiro, Brazil.

**YOUR TURN!**

Sasha makes art out of unexpected materials, like her staple gun portraits. What unusual materials can you use to make art? Take a walk around your house, looking for inspiration. Gather your materials and make your own unique masterpiece!

# SEONDEOK OF SILLA

## QUEEN

Circa 610–
February 17, 647
Korea

Seondeok of Silla was the first queen to rule one of the three kingdoms of Korea, after a long history of 26 kings.

## SUPERPOWERS
### INGENUITY, LEADERSHIP

★ A nobleman saw a falling star in the sky and told the people of Silla that it was a sign Seondeok's reign would soon fall. To prove she was there to stay, Seondeok made her own "star" by flying a burning kite over the kingdom.

★ She sent scholars to China to learn their customs and help build ties of friendship between the countries.

★ Her leadership brought a golden age of art, literature, and thought.

★ The "Star-Gazing Tower" created during her reign was one of the first observatories in Asia. It is still standing today.

# SERENA WILLIAMS
## TENNIS PLAYER
### Born September 26, 1981
### United States

Serena Williams has won 23 Grand Slam tournaments—those are the most prestigious tennis competitions in the world. She also earned four Olympic gold medals!

⭐ Serena was often the youngest to compete in tennis tournaments.

⭐ Growing up, she shared a bedroom with her four older sisters.

⭐ Serena created a foundation to build schools in Jamaica and Africa.

⭐ To push herself during a workout, she likes to listen to David Bowie's song "Fame."

⭐ Her favorite kitchen gadget is the toaster oven.

## SUPERPOWERS
### ENERGY, FOCUS

# SHAMSIA HASSANI

## GrAFFITI ARTIST

Born April 1988
Iran and Afghanistan

Shamsia Hassani is the first female graffiti artist in Afghanistan. Through her paintings, she advocates for women's rights in her country.

* Shamsia believes art can change people's minds, and that changing people's minds is a step toward changing the world.

* She paints on staircases, the walls of narrow streets, and even back alleys. She can finish a painting within minutes!

* Shamsia often paints women in her country to celebrate them, whether they're playing electric guitars or looking up at the sky wearing a full-body covering called a burka.

* Her name means "sun," which suits her because she loves sunny weather!

**SUPERPOWER**
*Self-expression*

# SHIRLEY CHISHOLM

## POLITICIAN

November 30, 1924–
January 1, 2005
United States

Shirley Chisholm was the
first woman and the first
Black person to run for
US president as part
of a major party.

**SUPERPOWERS** *PUBLIC SPEAKING, ASSERTIVENESS*

* Shirley spent the first seven years of her life with her grandmother in Barbados.

* Her first job after college was at a nursery school, teaching young children.

* In 1968, Shirley became the first Black woman elected to the US Congress.

* Her presidential slogan was "Unbought and Unbossed," to signal that her mission wasn't to achieve fame or fortune, but to serve the people, especially those who've been overlooked.

# SIMONE BILES

## GYMNAST

Born March 14, 1997
United States

Simone Biles is the most decorated American gymnast, with 32 medals at the world championships and seven at the Olympics.

## SUPERPOWERS
### PHYSICAL AND MENTAL STRENGTH

✳ Simone was adopted by her maternal grandparents when she was six years old.

✳ She trains in the gym for about 35 hours a week, around the same amount of time many people spend at their jobs.

✳ Simone takes medication for ADHD, which is a disorder that makes it hard to focus.

✳ She is a mental health advocate, and she isn't afraid to take breaks from gymnastics if she needs them.

✳ Many call her the "GOAT," or Greatest of All Time.

# SIMONE MANUEL
## SWIMMER
Born August 2, 1996
United States

**Simone Manuel was the first Black woman to win an Olympic gold medal in swimming. She did it at 19 years old!**

⭐ Starting at age nine, Simone joined her local swim team and began competing.

⭐ Many who know her call her "Swimone," a nickname for how natural she is in the water.

⭐ Growing up, Simone tried many activities, like soccer, volleyball, basketball, and dance, before finding the perfect fit.

⭐ In college, she studied communications and African and African American studies.

⭐ One of her favorite dishes is Cajun shrimp pasta.

## SUPERPOWERS
### ENTHUSIASM, FREESTYLE

# SKY BROWN
## skateboarder
Born July 7, 2008
Japan and
United Kingdom

At 13 years old, Sky Brown became the youngest member of the United Kingdom's first Olympic skateboarding team.

## SUPERPOWERS
### POSITIVITY, ATHLETICISM

⭐ Sky's dad was a skateboarder. Even as a baby, Sky liked to play on skateboards.

⭐ Sky has slick moves on concrete—and on the dance floor. She won *Dancing with the Stars: Juniors*.

⭐ She once plummeted 15 feet from a ramp while she was training, fracturing her skull and breaking her hand and her wrist.

⭐ She wants to show that girls can skate just as well as boys—and in her case, better!

# SOJOURNER TRUTH

## ABOLITIONIST & WOMEN'S RIGHTS ACTIVIST

### Circa 1797–November 26, 1883
### United States

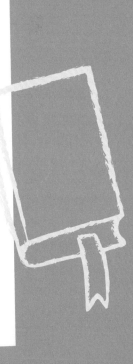

Sojourner Truth escaped slavery
and became an activist and writer
who spoke out about civil rights
and women's rights.

★ Born Isabella, she changed her name
to Sojourner, which means "the one
who travels."

★ When her son was sold off to Alabama,
Sojourner took his enslaver to court
and won. She knew it was illegal to sell
enslaved people across state lines. At the
time, it was very rare for a Black person
to win a case like this.

★ In 1851, she recited her famous speech
"Ain't I a Woman?" at the Ohio Women's
Rights Convention to argue that Black
women should have equal rights too.

★ Her first language was Dutch.

★ She published her life story in a book
titled *The Narrative of Sojourner Truth:
A Northern Slave*.

**SUPERPOWER**

*BOLDNESS*

# SOLVEIGA PAKŠTAITĖ

## INVENTOR & ENTREPRENEUR

Born May 21, 1992
Lithuania, Norway, and
United Kingdom

**Solveiga Pakštaitė founded a company of engineers and women scientists to make a label that turns bumpy when food expires.**

## SUPERPOWERS
### EMPATHY, INNOVATION

★ In college, Solveiga studied inclusive design to help solve everyday problems for people with disabilities.

★ She says the first step to making her idea work was hiring other people to help her. She realized she couldn't do it alone!

★ Solveiga started her company before she was 35 years old.

★ An important question Solveiga says young inventors should ask themselves before embarking on an idea is "Why hasn't this been done before?"

★ She has a rabbit named Bim.

# SONIA SOTOMAYOR
## SUPREME COURT JUSTICE
### Born June 25, 1954
### United States

Sonia Sotomayor is the daughter of immigrants and the first Latina judge to serve on the US Supreme Court.

⭐ Sonia wanted to become a lawyer and a judge after watching a show about lawyers on TV when she was 10 years old.

⭐ She played a major role in some of the country's most important legal cases, including *Obergefell v. Hodges*, which made same-sex marriage legal in all 50 states.

⭐ Sonia likes to cook, but says she is terrible at cooking the food from her Puerto Rican heritage.

⭐ She is a big Yankees fan.

**SUPERPOWERS** COMPASSION, CLEVERNESS

# SONITA ALIZADEH

## rapper

Born 1996
Afghanistan and Iran

Sonita Alizadeh wrote a song called "Brides for Sale," which went viral and won her a scholarship to study music in the United States.

**SUPERPOWERS** *courage, rap verses*

- When war broke out in Afghanistan, Sonita and her family walked hundreds of miles to flee to safety in Iran.

- Her parents first tried to sell her as a bride at 10 years old. Child marriage is a tradition in some countries, but Sonita used her music to speak out against it.

- Sonita's biggest influences are Iranian rapper Yas and American rapper Eminem.

- She once won $1,000 for writing a song encouraging young Afghans to vote.

# SOPHIA LOREN
## actor
### Born September 20, 1934
### Italy

**Sophia Loren rose to international fame for her glamorous style and award-winning performances.**

- Nicknamed "Toothpick," Sophia grew up in poverty in Naples, Italy, during World War II, when her family never had much to eat.

- Sophia got her big break at the Miss Italia Beauty Pageant after she was crowned Miss Elegance.

**SUPERPOWER** *POISE*

- She won an Academy Award for best actress for her role in *Two Women* as the courageous mother of a teenage girl during World War II.

- She has written two cookbooks.

# STACEY ABRAMS

## ACTIVIST & POLITICIAN

Born December 9, 1973
United States

Stacey Abrams became the first Black woman from a major party to run for governor of Georgia. Although she lost, she got more votes than any other Democrat in the state's history!

* Growing up, Stacey had five brothers and sisters and could often be found listening to hip-hop or watching *Star Trek*.

* In high school, she was named valedictorian for receiving the highest grades in her class.

* After she lost the race for governor, she worked hard over the next two years to register more than 800,000 people to vote in Georgia.

* Stacey has written more than 10 books!

* She collects teapots from around the world.

# STEFFI GRAF

## TENNIS PLAYER

Born June 14, 1969
Germany

Steffi Graf is one of the most celebrated tennis stars in the world. She's won 22 Grand Slam singles titles and an Olympic gold medal.

* Steffi won her first tennis tournament when she was six years old.

* She broke a record when she was voted German Sportsperson of the Year five times.

* When a fan shouted a marriage proposal at her during the 1996 Wimbledon match, Steffi joked, "How much money do you have?"

* More than 20 years ago, she founded Children for Tomorrow to support the mental health of children affected by violence and war.

# SUNI LEE

## GYMNAST

Born March 9, 2003
United States

**Sunisa "Suni" Lee's phenomenal routines earned her the all-around gold medal at the Tokyo Olympics in 2021.**

### ⚡ SUPERPOWERS
### *FLEXIBILITY, FOCUS*

* The uneven bar routine that Suni performed at the Tokyo Olympics was the most difficult in the world. She did four extremely advanced moves back to back.

* Suni became the first-ever Hmong American athlete to compete in the Olympics.

* When she was little, Suni practiced gymnastics in the backyard on a balance beam her father built for her.

* Suni was the first Asian American gymnast to win a gold medal in the all-around event.

# SYLVIA EARLE

## MARINE BIOLOGIST

### Born August 30, 1935
### United States

Sylvia Earle explores the deepest depths of the ocean and protects it from pollution and destruction.

**SUPERPOWER**
**ADVENTUROUSNESS**

* Sylvia loved to dive at night because there were lots of fish that couldn't be seen in the daytime, like moray eels.

* Sylvia led a team of aquanauts—people who live and work underwater.

* Sylvia wore a special suit and a huge, domed helmet that had four round windows to see through.

* Sylvia dived deeper than anyone had ever been without a rescue tether!

* She is often known as Her Deepness because of her underwater efforts.

# TAMMY DUCKWORTH
## senator
Born March 12, 1968
United States

**Tammy Duckworth is the first Asian American woman to be elected to Congress from the state of Illinois.**

**SUPERPOWERS** *GRIT, DETERMINATION*

+ Tammy lived in five countries before she graduated from high school: Singapore, Thailand, Indonesia, Cambodia, and the United States.

+ She joined the military and trained as a helicopter pilot. Her dad was a marine, and she wanted to follow his example.

+ Tammy was sent to Iraq in 2004. She lost both of her legs when her helicopter was attacked.

+ In 2018, she was the first person to give birth while serving as a US senator.

+ Her favorite song is "Purple Rain" by Prince.

# TANIA J. LEÓN FERRÁN

## COMPOSER & CONDUCTOR

Born May 14, 1943
Cuba and United States

Tania J. León Ferrán has traveled the world composing and conducting music.

Tania began training at the local music conservatory when she was four years old, thanks to her grandmother, who enrolled her.

Her music tells stories from history, including tales from her Cuban, African, Spanish, and Chinese ancestors.

She says she has to work twice as hard as male conductors to get the same amount of recognition.

Tania was the music director for *The Wiz* on Broadway.

# TANYARADZWA "TANYA" MUZINDA

## MOTOCROSS RIDER

Born April 30, 2004
Zimbabwe and United States

Tanyaradzwa "Tanya" Muzinda is the first woman to win a motocross championship in Zimbabwe.

✳ Tanya got her first motocross bike when she was five years old.

✳ Her mentor is an Italian motocross rider named Stefy Brau.

✳ The journey to motocross stardom has not been completely smooth. In 2017, Tanya fell from a 100-foot-high jump. She injured her hip and had to take a break from riding to heal.

✳ To further her career, Tanya and her family moved to Florida. She donates portions of her prize money to fund the education of girls in Zimbabwe.

# TAYLOR SWIFT
## SINGER-SONGWRITER
Born December 13, 1989
United States

**Taylor Swift is a world-famous singer-songwriter whose songs have topped the country and pop music charts.**

**SUPERPOWERS** *STORYTELLING, MUSICALITY*

* On Christmas morning when she was eight years old, Taylor unwrapped a very special gift: her first guitar.

* Taylor grew up on a Christmas tree farm in Pennsylvania. When she was 14, her family moved to Nashville, Tennessee, so Taylor could pursue her music career.

* Known for her vivid and personal lyrics, Taylor is the only female artist to win the Grammy Award for album of the year three times.

* She has two Scottish Fold cats, Meredith and Olivia, and a Ragdoll cat named Benjamin.

* Her favorite number is 13.

363

# TAYTU BETUL

## empress

Circa 1851–February 11, 1918
Ethiopia

Celebrated as "the Light of Ethiopia," Taytu Betul ruled the country alongside her husband, Emperor Menelik II, from 1889 to 1913.

**⚡SUPERPOWER**
**STRATEGIC THINKING**

+ Taytu could read and write in Amharic, which was rare for a woman at the time.

+ In the Battle of Adwa, she rode on horseback to the front lines to command thousands of soldiers to fight against Italian forces.

+ Taytu founded Addis Ababa, which is still Ethiopia's capital. During the end of her reign, she led the city into a period of technological advancement.

+ She liked to play chess and an instrument called the stringed begena. It sounds like a harp.

# TEGAN VINCENT-COOKE

## para Dressage rider

Born March 12, 2001
United Kingdom

Tegan Vincent-Cooke is an
aspiring Paralympian who
shares videos about what
it's like to be an athlete with
cerebral palsy.

### SUPERPOWERS
## HUMOR, HORSEBACK RIDING

+ Tegan has quadriplegic cerebral palsy, which sometimes
makes it hard for her to move her arms and legs.

+ Tegan and her horse spend hours practicing and performing
choreographed dance routines together. She calls her sport
"ballet on a horse."

+ Tegan posts fun videos on YouTube and TikTok about her
everyday life. She talks about everything from training in
the barn to what she plans on wearing to her birthday party.

+ She was inspired to start competing when she saw fellow
para horseback dressage rider Sophie Christiansen win
at the London Paralympics in 2012.

# TEMPLE GRANDIN

## PROFESSOR OF
## ANIMAL SCIENCES
### Born August 29, 1947
### United States

**Temple Grandin is a scientist and industrial designer who works to improve conditions for livestock and educate people about autism.**

 **SUPERPOWERS** *ANIMAL KNOWLEDGE, INNOVATION*

 Temple didn't speak until she was three and a half years old. She was later diagnosed with autism.

 She has written more than 60 scientific papers about animal behavior and was inducted into the Women's Hall of Fame in 2017.

 Her autism makes her sensitive to sound and touch. Her experiences help her understand how to help animals with similar sensitivities.

One of Temple's inventions was the "squeeze machine," a contraption that cradles animals closely to calm them. The machine has been adapted to help soothe some people with autism as well.

YOUR TURN!

Temple has invented solutions to help make animals' lives better. Design an invention for a cat or dog that would improve the pet's life.

# TEREZA LEE

## IMMIGRATION ACTIVIST

Born January 12, 1983
Brazil and United States

Tereza Lee is a pianist known as the original "DREAMer," a term that refers to a group of undocumented young people in the United States.

## SUPERPOWERS
### BRAVERY, PIANO SOLOS

* Tereza's parents are from South Korea, but she was born in Brazil. After the family moved to the United States, Tereza's dad told her they were undocumented immigrants.

* In high school, Tereza won a prominent music competition in Chicago. She wanted to attend a top music college but couldn't apply because she was undocumented.

* She told her story to Illinois senator Dick Durbin. It inspired him to draft the DREAM Act, a bill that would allow undocumented immigrants who were brought to the United States as children to become citizens.

* One of her favorite composers is Sergei Prokofiev.

# THEODORA OF LIECHTENSTEIN

## CONSERVATIONIST

Born November 20, 2004
Liechtenstein and Italy

Real-life princess Theodora of Liechtenstein founded the Green Teen Team to educate teens on the importance of conservation, especially for endangered tortoises.

* Because she comes from a royal family, Theodora grew up in a castle.

* When Theodora launched her foundation, the ceremony was opened by famous primatologist Jane Goodall.

* Theodora has accomplished many projects with the Green Teen Team, including building a protected habitat for turtles.

* She is a junior dressage rider and owns a stallion she calls Black Diamond.

## SUPERPOWER
### CAN-DO SPIRIT

# THOKOZILE MUWAMBA
## FIGHTER PILOT
### Born March 6, 1992
### Zambia

Thokozile Muwamba was the first female fighter pilot in Zambia.

+ In her first year as a university student studying math and science, Thokozile applied for the Zambian Air Force.

+ To become a fighter pilot, she had to undergo years of military training and then two years of flight training.

+ She has six siblings, and she's the third oldest.

+ Her aunt was a pilot and gave her advice on how to stay calm while flying.

# TONI MORRISON

## author

February 18, 1931–
August 5, 2019
United States

Toni Morrison wrote several award-winning books about the experiences of Black people in the United States.

## SUPERPOWERS
### VIVID WRITING, IMAGINATION

Toni saw an ad in the newspaper for a book editor job and ended up working for many years to help publish the works of great Black thinkers and activists.

In 1970, Toni released her first book, *The Bluest Eye*. It is about a young Black girl growing up during the Great Depression.

She also wrote children's books, like *Little Cloud* and *Lady Wind*, with her son Slade.

In 1993, she won the Nobel Prize for Literature.

Oprah's Book Club has featured Toni's books four times.

# TURIA PITT
## aTHLeTe & auTHor
### Born July 25, 1987
### Tahiti and Australia

Runner Turia Pitt became a motivational speaker after being injured in a wildfire while competing in a race.

- Turia decided to run an ultramarathon after she got her first engineering job. The race was 100 kilometers. That's 62 miles—a distance that usually takes an hour to drive!

- During the marathon, a sudden grassfire engulfed her, and doctors said she would never walk again.

- Turia lost seven fingers and had more than 200 medical procedures. She had to learn how to walk, talk, and feed herself again.

- Turia is a motivational speaker and an author. She's written five books and gives talks encouraging people to overcome the challenges in their lives.

- Her signature dish is a dessert: chocolate mint slices!

SUPERPOWER resilience

# VALERIE THOMAS

## astronomer & inventor

Born February 8, 1943
United States

Valerie Thomas invented the illusion transmitter in 1980. It is a technology still used in surgeries and TV sets today.

**SUPERPOWER** *CURIOSITY*

Valerie went to an all-girls high school that didn't see the value in teaching girls scientific subjects. That didn't stop her! She was one of two women in her class at her university who majored in physics.

After she graduated college, she got a job with NASA and worked on a satellite that could examine Earth's resources from space.

When Valerie first started at NASA, her job was in computer programming, but she'd never even seen a computer before—except in science fiction movies! She quickly learned everything she could about them.

After retiring from NASA, she became a substitute teacher.

# VIOLA DAVIS

## actor

Born August 11, 1965
United States

**Viola Davis is the only Black woman to win the top awards for acting in a TV show, movie, and Broadway play.**

 One of Viola's first experiences with acting was entering a local skit contest with her sisters at eight years old. They won!

 Viola studied theater in college and landed her first role on Broadway after she graduated.

 She once prepared for a seven-minute scene by writing a 50-page character biography.

 As of 2022, Viola is the most-nominated Black actress in the history of the Academy Awards.

 She's written a children's book called *Corduroy Takes a Bow.*

**YOUR TURN!**

Viola often gets into character by imagining all the details of her character's life. Practice being an actor like Viola and create a character. Come up with details about your character. Decide what their favorite food is, what kind of music they listen to, and what their biggest accomplishments are. Then think about how they talk, what hand gestures they make, and how they stand. Write a monologue as your character and act it out.

# VIOLA DESMOND
## entrepreneur & activist

July 6, 1914–
February 7, 1965
Canada

Viola Desmond opened Nova Scotia's first hair salon for Black women, but she didn't stop there. She also opened a beauty school that taught business skills.

**SUPERPOWER**
*BUSINESS SENSE*

★ Viola had 10 siblings!

★ Beauty schools in Canada wouldn't accept Viola because she was Black. She traveled to the US to train under well-known beauty entrepreneur Madam C. J. Walker.

★ In 1946, Viola challenged segregation by sitting in the front section of a theater. The police dragged her out and threw her in jail for a night.

★ In 2018, the Canadian government put her face on a $10 bill.

# VIOLETA PARRA
## COMPOSER & MUSICIAN
### October 4, 1917–
### February 5, 1967
### Chile

Called the Mother of Latin American Folk, Violeta Parra wrote and recorded songs dedicated to local music traditions.

⭐ Violeta's dad was a music teacher.

⭐ Violeta traveled across Chile to even the most remote areas with a recorder and a notebook to gather memories and songs passed down from generation to generation.

⭐ Her song "Gracias a la Vida" is one of the most covered Latin American songs in history. It is all about being thankful.

⭐ Violeta was also a sculptor, painter, and embroiderer. One of her tapestries was exhibited at the Louvre Museum in Paris after her death.

**SUPERPOWER**
*STORYTELLING*

# VIRGINIA HALL

## SPY

April 6, 1906–July 8, 1982
United States, United Kingdom, and France

**Virginia Hall was declared America's greatest female spy during World War II. Once, she escaped danger by disguising herself as an elderly milkmaid!**

## SUPERPOWERS *courage, intelligence*

 Virginia had jobs in Poland, Turkey, and Italy before her biggest mission—working as a spy in France during World War II. There she helped uncover valuable information about the war and relayed it to the British government.

 Virginia lost her leg from the knee down on a hunting trip when she was 27 years old. She used a prosthetic leg, which she lovingly named Cuthbert.

 During World War II, the Gestapo, or secret police of Nazi Germany, referred to Virginia as the "Limping Lady." She was always one step ahead of them.

* Virginia had a knack for languages. She could speak French, German, Italian, Spanish, and Russian.

Write a super-secret invisible spy note like Virginia would've done.

## MATERIALS NEEDED:

- Baking soda
- Water
- Cup
- Cotton swab or toothpick
- Grape juice

YOUR TURN!

## MAKE INVISIBLE INK:

1. Combine 2 tablespoons of baking soda and 2 tablespoons of water in a cup. Dip a cotton swab or toothpick in the mixture and write your message on a piece of paper. Let it dry.

2. Dip a new cotton swab or toothpick in grape juice and "paint" over the paper to reveal the secret message!

Berlin

London

Paris

Vichy

# VIVIAN MAIER

## PHOTOGRAPHER

February 1, 1926–
April 21, 2009
France and United States

Vivian Maier took more than 100,000 photographs of people on the street in her lifetime. Her pictures were not discovered until after her death.

**⚡SUPERPOWER**
*OBSERVATION*

★ Vivian worked as a nanny for 40 years, and she lived with the families she worked for.

★ She used a Rolleiflex camera to capture the moments in everyday life—like kids jumping rope or splashing in the water from a fire hydrant. Sometimes she snapped photos of herself in mirrors.

★ Her photography was discovered when she failed to pay the rent for her storage space and photo collectors bought her work.

★ Vivian spent most of her childhood in France and said she learned English from theater and plays.

# WANGARI MAATHAI
## ENVIRONMENTAL ACTIVIST
### April 1, 1940–September 25, 2011
### Kenya

Wangari Maathai founded the Green Belt Movement, whose members planted more than 51 million trees. She was the first African woman to earn the Nobel Peace Prize.

* Wangari started her environmental movement with just a few other women. They collected seeds from the forest and planted them in cans and pots.

* Her mother planted ideas of environmentalism in young Wangari's mind. As she gathered firewood, she called fig trees "trees of god" and explained that they helped protect people from landslides.

* Wangari wrote four books about the environment and her life.

* In her final effort to save trees, Wangari left a note saying she did not want to be buried in a wooden casket.

**SUPERPOWER**
**PERSISTENCE**

# WARSAN SHIRE

## POET

Born August 1, 1988
Somalia and United Kingdom

At 26 years old, Warsan Shire became the first
Young Poet Laureate of London.

## SUPERPOWERS

### DESCRIPTIVE WRITING, OUTSPOKENNESS

+ Warsan's parents were forced
to leave Somalia because war
broke out in their country.
Warsan was born in Kenya,
and she moved to London with
her parents as refugees.

+ She carries a small recorder
and uses it to capture her
family's stories. She turns
their laughter, memories, and
pain into thoughtful poems.

+ Her words were featured on
Beyoncé's album *Lemonade*.

+ Warsan's names mean
"good news" and "to gather
in one place."

# WILMA MANKILLER
## TRIBAL CHIEF
November 18, 1945–April 6, 2010
United States

In 1985, Wilma Mankiller became the first female head of the Cherokee Nation.

- Wilma grew up poor. Her family had no electricity, indoor plumbing, or telephone.

- When she decided to become an activist, Wilma's husband disapproved. She divorced him and continued pursuing her goals.

- Wilma founded the Community Development Department for the Cherokee Nation, helping secure running water for 200 families in a small town in Oklahoma.

- When a Native American art exhibit asked her to send a pair of shoes, she sent them her everyday walking shoes.

**SUPERPOWER**
**COMPASSION**

# WILMA RUDOLPH

## ATHLETE

June 23, 1940–
November 12, 1994
United States

At the 1960 Olympics, Wilma Rudolph was the first woman to win three gold medals, breaking world records and earning her the title of "the Fastest Woman in the World."

* Wilma was paralyzed by polio as a young child, and doctors said she would never walk again. With help from her family, Wilma recovered and began playing sports.

* Wilma had 21 brothers and sisters!

* Basketball was Wilma's first love—it was during a basketball tournament that Wilma met a track-and-field coach who convinced her to train as a runner.

* Her life story was turned into a movie in 1977.

SUPERPOWERS
SPEED, RESILIENCE

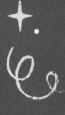

# WINONA LADUKE
## ACTIVIST & FARMER
Born August 18, 1959
United States

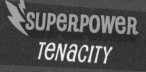
Winona LaDuke is an Ojibwe enrolled member advocating for Indigenous control of their homelands, resources, and practices. She even ran for president—twice!

✳ In the early 1990s, Winona organized a concert series with the music group Indigo Girls to help inform young people about Native issues.

✳ She spoke in front of the United Nations in Switzerland on how Indigenous land was being misused.

✳ Winona helped create the Indigenous Women's Network, which connects Indigenous women activists.

✳ Later on, she became a farmer. Winona has raised horses and grown rice.

# XIAN ZHANG

## orchestra conductor

Born 1973
China and United States

---

Xian Zhang is an accomplished orchestra conductor and the musical director of the New Jersey Symphony Orchestra.

⚡ **SUPERPOWER** *PASSION*

 ★ Xian Zhang's father built a piano for her when she was three years old because they weren't sold near where they lived.

★ When she first conducted an orchestral piece, *The Marriage of Figaro*, Xian Zhang was just 20 years old.

★ In addition to being the musical director at the New Jersey Symphony Orchestra, Xian Zhang travels the world as a guest conductor.

★ If she had not been a conductor, she would have liked to be an architect.

# XIYE BASTIDA

## CLIMATE ACTIVIST

Born April 18, 2002
Mexico and United States

Xiye Bastida organized a 600-person walkout at her high school demanding that governments take action against climate change.

* Xiye belongs to the Otomi Toltec, a nation of Indigenous people.

* She had to give up gymnastics to make time for her activism.

* Xiye moved from her small hometown in Mexico after a severe drought followed by floods. The streets turned to a "river of brown, brown water," she said.

* Her nickname at her college in Pennsylvania is "Climate Girl."

**SUPERPOWER**
**CONVICTION**

# XÓCHITL GUADALUPE CRUZ LÓPEZ

## INVENTOR

Born January 1, 2009
Mexico

Xóchitl Guadalupe Cruz López made waves when she invented a solar water heater at eight years old.

* Xóchitl noticed people were chopping down trees for firewood because water heaters were too expensive.

* The prototype for her solar-powered heater was made from plastic bottles and other trash she found.

* Xóchitl was the first kid to win a prestigious award given out to women scientists in Mexico.

* She is inspired by Polish physicist Marie Curie.

* She loves playing soccer and watching Harry Potter films.

**SUPERPOWER**
*PROBLEM-SOLVING*

# YAA ASANTEWAA

## warrior queen

Circa 1840–October 17, 1921
Ghana

Yaa Asantewaa led an army to fight against British soldiers invading the Asante kingdom.

* When British colonizers invaded Yaa's kingdom, many other leaders surrendered. "If you, the men of Asante, will not go forward, then we will," said Yaa. "We the women will."

* One of her duties as queen was guarding "the golden stool," which was an important symbol of power and history for her people.

* Yaa was a skilled farmer before she was named queen.

* Her army was defeated and she was exiled to the Seychelle Islands, never to see her land again. But the memory of her fighting spirit lives on in songs and stories.

**SUPERPOWERS**
*STAMINA, FEARLESSNESS*

# YOKY MATSUOKA

## ROBOTICS ENGINEER

Born circa 1972
Japan and
United States

Yoky Matsuoka was one of the first people to work at X, a top-secret research department at Google. She then started her own tech companies, Nest Labs and Yohana.

## SUPERPOWER  INGENUITY

* Yoky moved to the US at 16 to chase her dream of being a tennis player. She had to give it up when she kept getting hurt.

* After college, Yoky built mechanical arms that helped people learn to use their muscles after a stroke. She won a MacArthur Fellowship Grant for her work!

* One of Yoky's newer inventions is a personal assistant device created to help busy moms organize their lives.

* She lives with her husband, four children, and a pet pig.

# YOUNG JEAN LEE

## PLAYWRIGHT

Born May 30, 1974
South Korea
and United States

In 2018, Young Jean Lee became the first Asian American woman to have a play produced on Broadway.

* Young Jean moved from South Korea to a small town in Washington when she was two years old.

* She went to college in California to study English and became fascinated with Shakespeare's plays.

* Young Jean founded her own theater company to write experimental plays that explored topics like race and politics.

* To brainstorm ideas for plays, she observes what's going on around her and then starts with a question: "What's the last play in the world I would ever want to write?"

**SUPERPOWER**
**CREATIVE VISION**

# YUAN YUAN TAN
## Ballerina
Born February 14, 1977
China and United States

**Yuan Yuan Tan was the youngest principal dancer in the history of the San Francisco Ballet—and the first from Asia.**

- Yuan Yuan's mother wanted to send her to ballet school, but her father wanted her to be a doctor. They flipped a coin, and the rest is history!

- Yuan Yuan has danced the lead role in many famous ballets, including *Swan Lake* and *The Nutcracker*.

- If a coin hadn't decided her fate, Yuan Yuan says she would've been a fashion designer.

- Her mother auditioned to be a dancer herself, but Yuan Yuan's grandfather wouldn't allow her to pursue it. "I'm just an only child that fulfilled her dream," Yuan Yuan says.

# YUSRA MARDINI
## SWIMMER

Born March 5, 1998
Syria and Germany

In 2016, swimmer Yusra Mardini competed with the first refugee Olympic team.

## SUPERPOWERS
### SELFLESSNESS, DETERMINATION

⭐ Yusra started swimming at three years old. She says the sport saved her life.

⭐ After their home was destroyed by bombs in the Syrian War, Yusra and her sister fled to Greece by boat with a group of fellow refugees. When the boat broke down, the two jumped into the ocean and helped pull everyone to shore.

⭐ At age 19, Yusra was named the youngest Goodwill Ambassador by the United Nations. She uses her role to fight for refugees everywhere by sharing her story.

⭐ She wrote a book about her life story, which has been made into a movie!

# ZAHA HADID

## architect

October 31, 1950–
March 31, 2016
Iraq and United Kingdom

Zaha Hadid was the first woman
to receive the Royal Gold Medal
from the Royal Institute of
British Architects.

**SUPERPOWER**
**DYNAMIC DESIGNS**

⭐ By seven years old, Zaha had
decided she wanted to be an architect.

⭐ Known as Queen of the Curve, Zaha designed buildings
that featured eye-catching lines and arches.

⭐ Her legacy lives on in her buildings—fire stations,
museums, and even an aquatic center.

⭐ Her favorite color was black. She liked seeing
the color in different textures.

# ZENDAYA

## actor & singer

Born September 1, 1996
United States

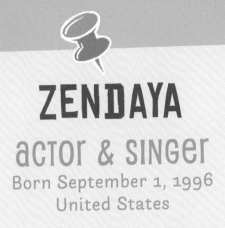

Zendaya is the youngest person to win an Emmy for lead actress in a drama.

## SUPERPOWERS
### CONFIDENCE, STYLE

★ Zendaya starred as backup dancer Rocky Blue on the Disney Channel show *Shake It Up!* Later, she was a real backup dancer in a commercial with Selena Gomez.

★ She was a fan of Spider-Man before joining the movie franchise as Michelle Jones Watson.

★ Her front teeth aren't sensitive to cold. She can bite right into ice cream!

★ Her full name is Zendaya Maree Stoermer Coleman.

# IMAGE CREDITS

11: Claudia Carieri (Makosinski), Sally Nixon (Parks), Camilla Ru (Williams), Cristina Portolano (Montoya), Eline Van Dam (Biles, Madonna), Ana Juan (Alonso), Sarah Madden (Lady Gaga). 13: Maya McKibbin (Lacquette), Kasia Bogdańska (Atwood), Lauwaart (Desmond). 15: Helena Morais Soares (Kahlo), Ren Capacio (Löpez), Paola Rollo (Cruz). 17: Sally Nixon (Tubman), Kiki Ljung (Hopper), Malin Rosenqvitz (Steinem). 19: Sofía Acosta (Nenquimo), Rocio Caputo (Pajón), Sonia Lazo (Miranda), Keisha Okafor (MC Soffia), Jeanne Detallante (Praeli), Paolo Rollo (Parra, Allende). 21: Sonia Lazo (Miranda), Annalisa Ventura (da Silva), Martina Paukova (Gabeira). 23: Paola Escobar (Salavarrieta), Rocio Caputo (Pajón), Mia Saine (Urrutia). 25: Monica Garwood (Boudicca), Ana Galvañ (Elizabeth I), Amanda Hall (Merian), Mia Saine (Jong), Ana Juan (Amaya), Sarah Mazzetti (Léon), Cristina Spanò (Montessori), Marta Signori (Callas). 27: Monica Garwood (Gentileschi), Gaia Stella (Aulenti), Abelle Hayford (Bardi). 29: Claudia Carieri (Curie), Annalisa Ventura (Mayer), Zosia Dzierzawska (Sendlerowa). 31: Giorgia Marras (Jin), Lieke Van Der Vorst (Bai), Stephanie Singleton (Duong), Xuan Loc Xuan (Voraakhom), Kiki Ljung (Seondeok), Eva Rust (Lee), Lisa Lanöe (Matsuoka). 33: Giorgia Marras (Jin), Lisk Feng (Dengping), Ping Zhu (Zhang). 35: Lieke Van Der Vorst (Bai), Jui Talukder (Barman), Paola Rollo (Khan). 37: Debora Guidi (DePrince), Bijou Karman (Wek), Gabrielle Tesafaye (Betul), Camilla Ru (Shire), Claire Idera (Iman), Noa Snir (Asantewaa), Sarah Madden (Kwali), T.S. Abe (Adichie), Naomi Anderson Subryan (Govera), Helena Morais Soares (Makeba), Sharee Miller (Bushell), Alice Barberini (Wamariya), Thandiwe Tshabalala (Maathai), Data Oruwari (Kosgei). 39: Thandiwe Tshabalala (Maathai), Data Oruwari (Kosgei), Monica Ahanonu (Nyong'o). 41: Jonell Joshua (Aguebor-Ekperuoh), T.S. Abe (Adichie), Sarah Madden (Kwali). 43: Annalisa Ventura (Irwin), Karyn Lee (Arora), Angela Acevedo Perez (Telford), Kathrin Honesta (Watson), Camelia Pham (Zhang), Monica Garwood (Wake). 45: Angela Acevedo Perez (Telford), Karyn Lee (Arora), Camelia Pham (Zhang). 48: Kirkor Minassian Collection (tablet), Sarah Mazzetti (Hortensia), Kiki Ljung (Cleopatra). 49: Monica Garwood (Boudicca), Kiki Ljung (Seondeok). 50: Ana Galvañ (Elizabeth I), Marijke Buurlage (Catherine the Great), Library of Congress Prints and Photographs Division (French Revolution), Elisabetta Stoinich (Lovelace). 51: Sally Nixon (Tubman), Library of Congress Brady-Handy Collection (Civil War), Claudia Carieri (Curie). 52: US Army Signal Corps. (WWI), Library of Congress Prints and Photographs Division (Russian Revolution), Library of Congress Bain Collection (Women's Suffrage), Tyla Mason (Baker). 53: Dorothea Lange (Great Depression), Giulia Flamini (Earhart), Helena Morais Soares (Kahlo), Toni Frissell Collection (WWII). 54: Zosia Dzierzanska (Peel), Marta Signori (Lamarr), Ana Juan (Alonso), Library of Congress Prints and Photographs Division (Korean War). 55: Library of Congress Bernard Gotfryd Photograph Collection (Vietnam War), Sally Nixon (Parks), NASA (Sputnik), Giulia Tomai (Bridges), Emmanuelle Walker (Goodall), NASA (Moon landing). 56: Emmanuelle Walker (King), Thandiwe Tshabalala (Maathai), Alexandra Bowman (Mankiller). 57: T.S. Abe (Winfrey), Defense Media Activity (Berlin Wall), Alexandra Bowman (Jemison), Eleanor Davis (Ginsburg). 58: Sophie Cunningham (Lee), Elenia Beretta (Merkel), Courtesy Barack Obama Presidential Library (photo), Sara Bondi (Yousafzai). 59: Pau Zamro (Thunberg), Nicole Miles (Harris), Kate Prior (Brown), Keturah Ariel (Gorman), United States Mint (Angelou quarter). 63: Elisabetta Stoinich (illustration), Margaret Sarah Carpenter (painting). 64: Camille de Cussac. 65: Giulia Tomai. 66: Bijou Karman. 67: Taylor McManus. 68: Cristina Portolano. 69: Martina Paukova. 71: Helen Li (illustration), Apeda Studio New York - Collection Solax (photo). 72: Juliette Léveillé. 73: Ana Juan. 74: Kim Holt. 75: Salini Perera. 77: Keturah Ariel (illustration), Invision (photo). 78: Geraldine Sy. 79: Giulia Flamini. 80: Lindsey Rendell for *Peppermint* magazine. 81: Angela Acevedo Perez. 82: Eline Van Dam. 83: Kelsee Thomas. 84: Zosia Dzierzanska. 85: Katelun C. Brewster. 86: Karyn Lee. 87: Claudia Carieri. 88: Toni D. Chambers. 89: Alice Piaggio. 91: Johnalynn Holland (illustration), Associated Press (photo). 92: Fanny Blanc. 93: Olivia Fields. 94: Monica Garwood. 95: Kate Prior. 96: Paolo Rollo. 97: Justine Lecouffe. 98: Kelsee Thomas. 99: Marta Signori. 100: Jing Li. 101: Adesewa Adekoya. 103: Jordan Strauss/Invision/ AP (photo), Tatheer Syeda (illustration). 104: Amari Mitnaul. 105: Cristina Portolano. 107: Charles G.Y. King, © National Portrait Gallery, London (photo), Barbara Dziadosz (illustration). 108: Toni D. Chambers. 109: Kim Holt. 110: Eline Van Dam. 111: Emmanuelle Walker. 112: Annalisa Ventura. 113: Jiaqi Wang. 114: Monica Garwood. 115: T.S. Abe. 116: Marylou Faure. 117: Maya McKibbin. 118: Data Oruwari. 119: Ana Juan. 120: Ana Juan. 121: Maïté Franchi. 122: Sonia Lazo. 123: Marijke Buurlage. 124: Ping Zhu. 125: Lydia Mba. 126: T.S. Abe. 127: Salini Perera 128: Cozbi A. Cabrera. 129: Trudi-Ann Hemans. 130: Cristina Spanò. 131: Cristina Amodeo. 133: Nicole Miles (illustration), Arnold Turner/Invision/AP (photo). 134: Alice Barberini. 135: Kiki Ljung. 136: Lydia Mba. 137: Elenia Beretta. 138: Claudia Carieri. 139: Fanesha Fabre. 140: Associated Press 141: Elisa Seitzinger. 142: Monet Kifner. 143: Petra Braun. 144: Monica Ahanonu. 145: Josefina Schargorodsky. 146: Lizzy Stewart. 147: Jennifer M. Potter. 148: Ana Galvañ. 149: Bodil Jane. 150: Eleni Debo. 151: Paola Rollo. 152: Mia Saine. 153: Noa Snir. 154: Alicia Robinson. 155: Dalila Rovazzani. 156: Associated Press. 157: Helena Morais Soares (illustration), Associated Press (photo). 158: Gosia Herba. 159: Adriana Bellet. 160: Gaia Stella. 161: Ana Juan. 162: Laura Perez. 163: Alleanna Harris. 164: Nan Lawson. 165: Malin Rosenqvitz. 166: Decue Wu. 167: Kiki Ljung. 168: Kathrin Honesta. 169: Pau Zamro. 170: Sally Nixon. 171: Eleni Kalorkoti. 173: Associated Press (photo), Sabrena Khadija (illustration). 174: Marta Signori. 175: Monica Garwood. 177: DeAndra Hodge (illustration), Associated Press (photo). 178: Riikka Sormunen. 179: Saniyyah Zahid. 180: Adriana Bellet. 181: Claire Idera. 182: Taylor McManus. 183: Zosia Dzierzawska. 185: Paolo Rollo (illustration), Associated Press (photo). 186: Cristina Amodeo. 187: Naki Narh. 188: Naomi Silverio. 189: Pau Zamro. 190: Sophia Martineck. 191: Emmanuelle Walker. 192: Veronica Ruffato. 193: Amy Phelps. 195: AP Images for U by Kotex (photo), Alexandra Bowman (illustration). 196: Kathrin Honesta. 197: Marijke Buurlage. 198: Cari Vander Yacht. 199: Tyla Mason. 200: Simone Martin-Newberry. 201: Renike. 203: Mira Miroslavova (illustration), Associated Press (photo). 204: Barbara Dziadosz. 205: Acacia Rodriguez. 206: Nicole Miles. 207: Monica Mikai. 208: Cristina Portolano. 209: Martina Paukova. 210: Helen Li. 211: Maya Ealey. 212: June Tien. 213: Xuan Loc Xuan. 215: Xuan Loc Xuan (illustration), Lillian Suwnrumpha/AFP via Getty Images (photo). 216: Keturah Ariel. 217: Sarah Madden. 218: Sarah Madden. 219: Lieke Van Der Vorst. 220: Alice Piaggio. 221: Alice Barberini. 222: Nicole Miles. 223: Sarah Mazzetti. 224: Sarah Loulendo. 225: Thandiwe Tshabalala. 226: Noa Snir. 227: Abelle Hayford. 228: Kim Holt. 229: Gosia Herba. 230: Vanessa Lovegrove. 231: Jeanne Detallante. 232: Camilla Perkins. 233: Sarah Wilkins. 235: Goldman Environmental Prize (photo), Sarah Loulendo (illustration). 236: Jennifer M. Potter. 237: Lisk Feng. 238: Monica Ahanonu. 239: Cristina Spanò. 240: Laura Junger. 241: Barbara Dziadosz. 242: Eline Van Dam. 243: Alexandra Bowman. 245: Sara Bondi (illustration), Associated Press (photo). 246: Nicole Miles. 247: Kate Prior. 248: Kasia Bogdańska. 249: Édith Carron. 250: Camelia Pham. 251: Cristina Spanò. 253: Associated Press (photo), Marta Signori (illustration). 254: Annalisa Ventura. 255: Mia Saine. 256: Cristina Spanò. 257: Gaia Stella. 258: Amanda Hall. 259: Rocio Caputo. 260: Claudia Carieri. 261: Lizzy Stewart. 263: Elena de Santi (illustration), Associated Press (photo). 264: Kesiha Okafor. 265: Naki Narh. 266: Annalisa Ventura. 267: Martina Paukova. 268: Elizabeth Baddeley. 269: Alice Beniero. 270: Elisabetta Stoinich. 271: Giorgia Marras. 272: Cristina Portolano. 273: Giulia Flamini. 274: Thandiwe Tshabalala. 275: Martina Paukova. 276: Keisha Okafor. 277: Kim Holt. 278: Alice Barberini. 279: Marina Muun. 281: Debora Guidi (illustration), Associated Press (photo). 282: Lily Kim Qian. 283: Salini Perera. 284: Ronique Ellis. 285: Sarah Wilkins. 286: Eva Rust. 287: Meel Tamphanon. 288: Helena Morais Soares. 289: Ping Zhu. 291: Kylie Akia Erwin (illustration), Kendy Joseph (photo). 292: Maliha Abidi. 293: Julia Kuo. 294: Veronica Carratello. 295: Monica Garwood. 296: Sharee Miller. 297: Jeanetta Gonzales. 299: Danielle Elysse Mann (illustration), Associated Press (photo). 300: Eleni Kalorkoti. 301: Zara Picken. 302: Sofía Acosta. 303: Decue Wu. 304: T.S. Abe. 305: Yevhenia Haidamaka. 306: Tatsiana Burgaud. 307: Joelle Avelino. 308: Valencia Spates. 309: Jennifer M. Potter. 310: T.S. Abe. 311: Jacquelyn B. Moore. 312: Naomi Anderson-Subryan. 313: Sarah Mazzetti. 314: Kate Prior. 315: Onyinye Iwu. 317: Paola Escobar (illustration), José María Espinosa (painting). 318: Kylie Akia Erwin. 319: Priya Kuriyan. 320: Jui Talukder. 321: Giorgia Marras. 322: Sarah Wilkins. 323: Tamiki. 324: Stephanie Singleton. 325: Jestenia Southerland. 326: Sally Nixon. 327: Sasha Kolesnik. 328: Liekeland. 329: Sally Caulwell. 330: Aisha Akeju. 331: Fanesha Fabre. 332: Liekeland. 333: Eleanor Davis. 335: Jeanetta Gonzales (illustration), Jordan Strauss/Invision/AP (photo). 336: Giulia Tomai. 337: Sharee Miller. 338: Jonell Joshua. 339: Clara Dupré. 340: Carmen Casado. 341: Lisk Feng. 343: Tiffany Baker (illustration), Kai Kuusisto (photo). 344: Kiki Ljung. 345: Camilla Ru. 346: Cristina Portolano. 347: Olivia Fields. 348: Eline Van Dam. 349: Danielle Elysse Mann. 350: Kate Prior. 351: Cristina Amodeo. 352: Thaiz Zafalon. 353: Kathrin Honesta. 354: Samidha Gunjal. 355: Marta Signori. 356: Kelsee Thomas. 357: Giulia Flamini. 358: Danielle Elysse Mann. 359: Geraldine Sy. 360: Alessandra De Cristofaro. 361: Keisha Morris. 362: Dominique Ramsey. 363: Anna Dixon. 364: Gabrielle Tesafaye. 365: DeAndra Hodge. 367: Beatrice Cerocchi (illustration), Associated Press (photo). 368: Sophie Cunningham. 369: Sofia Cavallari. 370: Ashleigh Corrin. 371: Noa Denmon. 372: Léa Taillefert-Rolland. 373: Camilla Perkins. 375: Johnalynn Holland (illustration), Jordan Strauss/Invision/AP (photo). 376: Lauwaart. 377: Paola Rollo. 379: Dalila Rovazzani (illustration), Central Intelligence Agency (photo). 380: Sara Olmos. 381: Thandiwe Tshabalala. 382: Camilla Ru. 383: Alexandra Bowman. 384: Alice Barberini. 385: Debora Islas. 386: Camelia Pham. 387: Sally Deng. 388: Ren Capacio. 389: Noa Snir. 390: Lisa Lanöe. 391: Salini Perera. 392: Petra Braun. 393: Jessica Cooper. 394: Noa Snir. 395: Tyler Mishá Barnett.

# MORE FROM REBEL GIRLS

# LISTEN TO MORE EMPOWERING STORIES ON THE REBEL GIRLS APP!

Download the app to listen to beloved Rebel Girls stories, as well as brand-new tales of extraordinary women. Filled with the adventures and accomplishments of women from around the world and throughout history, the Rebel Girls app is designed to entertain, inspire, and build confidence in listeners everywhere. There are 31 QR codes in this book that will whisk you away on audio adventures. Can you find them?

# ABOUT REBEL GIRLS

REBEL GIRLS is a global, multi-platform empowerment brand dedicated to helping raise the most inspired and confident generation of girls through content, experiences, products, and community. Originating from an international best-selling children's book, Rebel Girls amplifies stories of real-life women throughout history, geography, and field of excellence. With a growing community of nearly 20 million self-identified Rebel Girls spanning more than 100 countries, the brand engages with Generation Alpha through its book series, award-winning podcast, events, and merchandise. With the 2021 launch of the Rebel Girls app, the company has created a flagship destination for girls to explore a wondrous world filled with inspiring true stories of extraordinary women.

As a B Corp, we're part of a global community of businesses that meets high standards of social and environmental impact.

Join the Rebel Girls' community:
- Facebook: facebook.com/rebelgirls
- Instagram: @rebelgirls
- Twitter: @rebelgirlsbook
- TikTok: @rebelgirlsbook
- Web: rebelgirls.com
- Podcast: rebelgirls.com/podcast
- App: rebelgirls.com/app

If you liked this book, please take a moment to review it wherever you prefer!